Private Pilot Blueprint

EDITION 3

Jason Schappert, CFII

MzeroA (pronounced M-zero-A) is an online ground school and flight training community that helps thousands of members per month pass their FAA knowledge tests, checkrides, and helps those members to keep learning after obtaining their certificates and ratings. We believe "A Good Pilot Is Always Learning" is truly a statement to live by. You can learn more about the benefits of our Online Ground School by visiting MzeroA.com.

Copyright © 2024 Gulfstream Media LLC
DBA MzeroA.com
Private Pilot Blueprint
by Jason Schappert

All rights reserved. No part of this publication may be reproduced, distributed, or transmitted in any form or by any means, including photocopying, recording, or other electronic or mechanical methods, without the express written permission of the publisher, except for the use of brief quotations in critical reviews and other noncommercial uses as permitted by copyright law.

ISBN-10: 8985397024
ISBN-13: 979-8985397024

A Note From The Author

What if we showed up every day to be better versions of ourselves? Gaining more each day — more knowledge, understanding, and real-world skills. This is my reason for this book and MzeroA.com. Everyday we ask: what can we do today to create safer, smarter pilots?

My goal is to keep you inspired in pursuing Aviation Mastery. Mastery in aviation, or any pursuit, has no finish line. This book is filled with motivational messages, the science of learning and aviation safety from my 10,000+ hours as a pilot and flight instructor.

When I started, I never imagined we'd be here today. My dream was to be a military aviator, specifically flying the USAF F15-E. My parents owned a pest control business, and my mom was a nurse. I didn't come from an aviation family, and my grades were poor. My mother loves to share stories of my elementary school report card full of C's and D's, with a note that read: "Jason won't stop talking. He'll talk to anyone. I believe he would talk to the window if it would talk back!" The only perfect grade I received that year was on a final project titled "Pilot," earning a full score, saving my GPA.

At 12, my father did pest control for a local realtor who offered me a flight lesson in exchange. It was a deal, and I was hooked!

At 15, we got serious with my lessons. Dad began pressure washing for extra money, and Mom picked up extra shifts. I worked at a paintball field for $40 a day in cash. It all went towards my dream.

Everyone's journey looks different. No matter where you are in your aviation journey, there is more to be done and to learn. Whether you're a prospective student pilot or a rusty pilot, approach this book with a student mindset. We say a good pilot is always learning. It's a statement to live by. Thank you for embarking on this journey towards Aviation Mastery and for making MzeroA one of the best!

Jason Schappert

Praise For This Book

Did you know that this book is available on audible.com? Many learners find it helpful to use this audio version so that they can take the book with them on the road, in the car, in the gym and simply when working around the house.

All the same valuable information can be delivered right to your ears, saving you time and giving you even more opportunity to learn and study throughout the day.

Don't take our word for it, check out these 5 star reviews given by satisfied customers.

"The most essential and valuable tool in a pilot's flight bag is MzeroA. It is required for all my students."
- Larry Diamond, CFII

How to Use This Book

Let this book be your guide. It's everything I wish I had before I started my training. Each chapter walks you through essential steps and knowledge needed to become a successful pilot. Start at the beginning, take your time, and absorb the information. Use the tips and insights to save time, money, and avoid common pitfalls.

You'll find practical advice, real-world scenarios, and expert tips to navigate your training with confidence. Refer to this book often, as a roadmap for your journey. Make notes, highlight key points, and revisit chapters as needed. This compact book is full of valuable information and is easy to take with you anywhere you go. Download the audiobook from Audible or the App Store.

Remember, you are not alone in this journey. The MzeroA Nation is a vibrant community of pilots and learners. Connect with fellow aviators through our forums, social media groups, and webinars. The MzeroA community supports you, answers your questions, and shares in your triumphs.

Embrace the process, stay curious, and always keep learning. Welcome to the MzeroA family—we're excited to be part of your aviation journey.

Contact us with ANY checkride questions. We are here to help!
Support@MzeroA.com | 855-737-1200

-**Jason Schappert**
Founder, MzeroA

Disclaimer

Our dedicated MzeroA team diligently collaborates each day to maintain the accuracy, accessibility, and timeliness of this book and all our educational materials. Our mission at MzeroA is to provide you with the finest study resources available.

At the time of publication, the information within this guide was thoroughly researched and verified for accuracy. However, it's important to acknowledge that regulations, FAA testing procedures, and technological advancements evolve continuously. Consequently, some information may become outdated in the months and years following publication.

Rest assured, we are committed to regularly updating and revising our study materials to reflect these changes. If you happen to identify an error, please don't hesitate to reach out to us. Keeping our resources current is a collaborative effort, and as a valued member of the MzeroA community, your input is invaluable.

In aviation, change is the only constant, as the saying goes. Therefore, we encourage you to utilize the latest editions of FAA resources, as they are regularly refreshed.

Your decision to entrust MzeroA with your Private Pilot Blueprint preparation signifies more than just confidence — it signifies a partnership that we deeply cherish. Together, we are dedicated to ensuring your success on this monumental journey. Thank you for allowing us to be a part of realizing your dreams!

Acknowledgements

To the exceptional team at MzeroA, whose unwavering dedication and expertise have brought this latest edition of Pass Your Private Pilot Blueprint to fruition. Your collective commitment to excellence and innovation sets a standard that inspires us all.

Together, we have redefined what it means to deliver top-tier educational materials. Your passion, drive, and relentless pursuit of perfection have made MzeroA synonymous with quality and reliability.

Thank you for your steadfast dedication to our mission and for being the backbone of our success.

Table of Contents

CHAPTER	PAGE
1. Welcome to the World of Aviation!	15
2. Set up for Success	33
3. Getting Started	53
4. The Journey	63
5. Keys to the Knowledge Test	79
6. Pass your Checkride	87
7. The Sky's the Limit	97
8. The Aviation Mastery Method	109
Appendix: Aviation Acronyms	114

CHAPTER 1
WELCOME TO THE WORLD OF AVIATION!

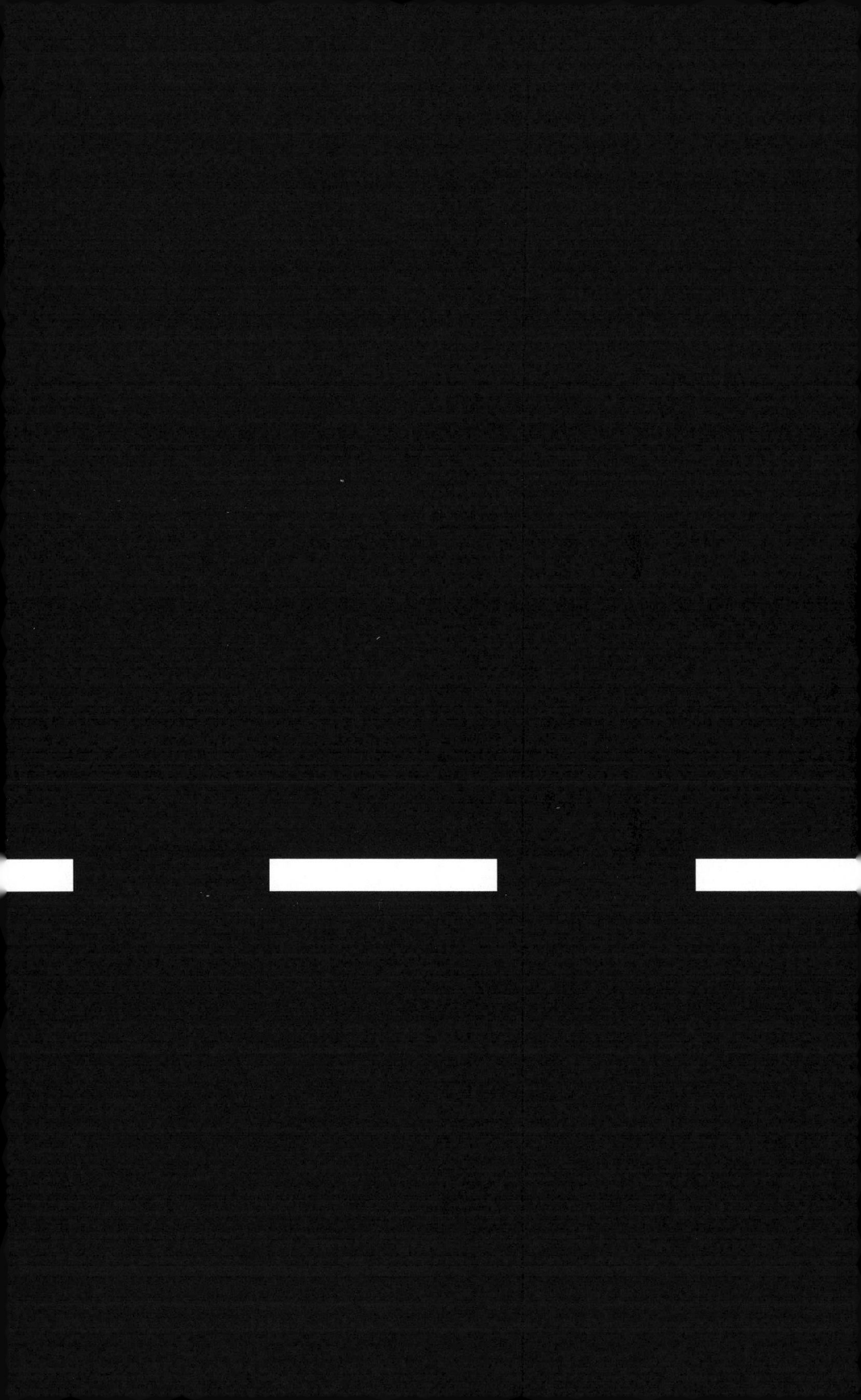

CHAPTER 1
Welcome to the World of Aviation!

"Once you have tasted flight, you will forever walk the Earth with your eyes turned skyward, for there you have been, and there you will always long to return."

— Leonardo da Vinci

Being a pilot is truly a rewarding experience. Many pilots enjoy flying as an exciting and successful career, while other pilots simply appreciate it as a hobby. As you'll see throughout this book, and on your journey to become a pilot, aviation offers unlimited opportunities.

Congratulations on pursuing your dreams and joining our amazing aviation community! You probably got this book because you are just getting started and you aren't really sure how to go about it, that's okay, we have all been there!

Reading the Private Pilot Blueprint is a great first step in getting started. This book will share everything the MzeroA team and I wished someone would have told us when getting started in aviation, especially how to save time and money. You will also gain a thorough overview of the process of becoming a pilot and tips from the experts on how to be successful in your training. Training to be a pilot may seem like an unattainable goal at the beginning, but you can do it! Keep reading to find out how to make it happen. Remember that you are not alone, you now have an outstanding MzeroA family and aviation community supporting you!

At MzeroA, we are eager to guide you and share our passion for aviation. Together, along with this book, our industry leading online ground school, aviation mastery study method, flight instructor support and community you have all you need to become a safe real-world pilot and find success in your aviation journey!

As you begin your journey to become a pilot, you will initially find you have more questions than answers. Don't worry; I felt the same way when I was getting started. You'll learn many new terms and acronyms, and at times may think that pilots seem to speak in a different language. You may wonder, can I do this? Where do I start? Is it safe? How long is it going to take and maybe even more importantly, how much is this all going to cost? These questions are very normal and MzeroA has answers and solutions for you. However, your dreams can only become reality if you believe them.

Imagine yourself in that airplane flying overhead, because that can be you in the future! With this book and the MzeroA Online Ground School, we will address all your questions and offer a proven method used daily by thousands to become successful pilots.

GETTING STARTED AS A PILOT

In order to become a pilot, you must earn your pilot's certificate. The Private Pilot Certificate is the starting point for most aspiring pilots.

What exactly is a private pilot? It's someone who holds a pilot certificate and is limited to flying an airplane for pleasure or travel with friends and family. A private pilot can not fly for compensation or hire. Basically, you can't charge people to fly them. Flying for compensation requires a different pilot certificate which we'll talk about later.

First things first, there are some eligibility requirements set by the Federal Aviation Administration (FAA) to become a private pilot. You must:

- Be at least 17 years of age.
- Be able to read, speak, write, and understand the English language.
- Complete private pilot ground school training, earn an endorsement of completion and pass the FAA Knowledge Test.
- Hold a valid medical certificate from an Aviation Medical Examiner (AME).
- Meet the aeronautical experience outlined by the FAA, earn an endorsement, and pass the practical test.

Many people believe that to get started working on their private pilot, they simply need to find a flight school and start flying lessons right away. I wish someone had told me to follow this sequence to save time and money when earning your certificate:

1. **Complete private pilot ground school.**
2. **Earn your required FAA medical certificate.**
3. **Pass the FAA Knowledge Test.**
4. **Find a flight school and start flying lessons.**
5. **Pass your FAA Practical Test, referred to as a checkride.**

This is one of my best kept secrets in saving time and money in earning your certificate.

Why do I consider this order to be so important? Because the airplane is a very expensive classroom. I get it, you just want to go fly... it is fun! Yet, many people don't realize that the airplane is the place to apply and practice what you learn during your ground school. The more knowledge you gain on the ground, the more effective your flight training will be in the air. Flight training is the most expensive part of obtaining your certificate. When you fly with your instructor, you pay the flight school by the hour for training. You want to focus on learning to fly the airplane instead of concepts and ground knowledge. Ground school work can be learned online and at home from your sofa where you aren't getting charged airplane fees. This allows you to be more efficient in your flight training and save money. I personally would have saved a lot of time and money on my training If I would have completed my ground school before starting my flight training, not the other way around.

Another important aspect that we always encourage the MzeroA Online Ground School Members to do, is to earn their FAA medical certificate from an Aviation Medical Examiner (AME) as soon as possible. You may be thinking, why do I need my medical certificate before I start my flight training? Well, with over 15 years of mentoring hundreds of thousands of pilots, we have seen time and time again where a learner completes the ground school, starts their flight training and doesn't realize until it's time to solo (and several thousand dollars into their flight training) that they have an issue such as high blood pressure or some other common medical condition. While you can still possibly earn your FAA medical certificate, it just takes a little more time and effort working with your FAA medical examiner.

Therefore, we strongly recommend earning your FAA medical certificate early on, just in case there are any issues that need to be documented and worked through with your FAA medical examiner or family physician. The key in saving time and money is to be as prepared as possible before you start your flight training.

If you try to do all your flight training without completing some sort of ground school, you are doing yourself a disservice. It is a well known statement that "for every hour you spend on the ground, you save two hours in the air." Flying is the fun part and all pilots feel that way. During your one hour lesson that costs you over $100 you will work to improve your stick and rudder skills. Don't let the stress of still trying to learn crucial topics like airspace, textual/physical weather, rules and regulations, flight planning and more get in the way of a productive flight lesson.

I also firmly believe that students should not get in the airplane without having a solid foundation and comprehension on the how, why, where, and what is happening to the aircraft. That foundation is built on the ground.

When I was a young kid, I decided that I wanted to become a pilot so I went to our local flight school and started flight lessons. Nobody ever told me what ground school was, nor even mentioned something called a FAA Knowledge Test. So I did ALL my flight training and met every single flight requirement. When I thought I checked all the boxes and requirements to take my private pilot checkride, my instructor said "Jason, you can't take your checkride yet, you haven't passed the written test!" I looked at my instructor and literally said "Umm...What's a written test?" You can only imagine the instructor's face at that moment. Rather than taking my checkride when I planned, I had to take two months off from flying to focus on my ground studies and pass my written test. That's two months that I could have been a private pilot and two months I could have been working towards another rating. The world is funny; now look what I do for a living!

As an seasoned instructor, I always say that a "dream student pilot" is the one who starts flying lessons when they already have completed the ground school from a reputable course (so the flight instructor knows they avoided rote memorization and actually know how to apply the aviation knowledge), hold their medical certificate and passed their knowledge test!

AVOIDING COMMON STUDENT PILOT PITFALLS

When we start a new journey, sometimes we don't know what we don't know.

If you want to avoid common mistakes and be successful while saving time and money, **find someone who has achieved the results you want and follow their steps!** MzeroA has one of the largest student pilot communities, and has helped hundreds of thousands of pilots achieve their aviation dreams for over 15 years. All you need to do is model those who have gone before you, and have achieved the success you desire.

We'd love for you to join our family, become a member of the MzeroA community and let the MzeroA team guide and help you avoid common student pilot pitfalls and errors while mentoring you to achieve your aviation goals. Everything you need to know to become a safe real-world pilot is in the MzeroA Online Ground School. Below is the website to access it for FREE for 2 weeks. You are welcome to use and share this free link with anyone you know could use some guidance and help in becoming a pilot!

Go to: www.MzeroATrial.com or scan the QR code below!

Another common pitfall is to start your flight training in an airplane that flies faster than a normal trainer. We all want to fly super cool airplanes with the latest instruments and technology. However, when it comes to flying, the goal is to "stay ahead of the airplane" and statistics show that student pilots who first start flight training with high performance aircraft have a hard time doing so in fast airplanes. They often need more flight hours to become proficient and earn their certificate. There is a big difference in decision making when flying at 90 knots versus flying at 160 knots. My recommendation is to start with slower airplanes geared towards training, and then after you have logged a good amount of flight hours and if your financial situation allows, go fly the fast and cool airplanes!

You may have a goal to fly a large commercial airplane, but when first starting out, most learners will fly two or four seat training aircraft. Learner is the term that the FAA uses for students or someone learning to fly. Flying smaller, less complex aircraft also allows you to focus more on the fundamentals of flight training. Aviation is all about building a strong foundation. As your experience, credentials and flight hours increase, you will find the opportunity to fly larger aircraft if you so choose. Along this journey, you'll learn about weather, aerodynamics, rules and regulations, airspace, and more. All of this knowledge is necessary for all pilots whether flying small or large aircraft.

Before long, you will feel like a pro at using all the aviation terms and acronyms commonly used. You can find a list of some common aviation acronyms at the end of this book to help get you started.

REQUIREMENTS TO EARN YOUR CERTIFICATE

As mentioned before, earning a Private Pilot Certificate requires the learner to pass two FAA exams: the Knowledge Test and The Practical Test. The Knowledge Test is a computer based multiple choice test with 60 questions and is commonly referred to as the written test. The Practical Test includes both an oral and flight portion. Most pilots use the term checkride instead of Practical Test. Now, before you become intimidated, your ground and flight training are designed to make sure you are more than prepared for all of this testing. Our goal at MzeroA is to prepare safe-real world pilots. Thus, our course is the most comprehensive course on the market, teaching pilots well beyond minimum FAA standards. Our goal is not only to help you pass your FAA exams with flying colors, but most importantly, thoroughly prepare you for real world flying. When everyone else hits the panic button and loses confidence while flying because they used rote memorization to earn their certificate, our MzeroA members know exactly **what to do, when to do it, and how to do it!**

Ground lessons through the MzeroA program are broken up into sections which will complement what you'll see, learn, and experience in the airplane. This gives you an added edge in your learning.

Along with many acronyms, you will become familiar with new terms in aviation. "Solo" and "dual" are two terms that you will need to know. Solo flying time is exactly how it sounds: time you spend flying by yourself, without your instructor. Dual flying is the flight hours spent with your instructor. The specific hour requirement of each is mandated by the FAA. You'll spend much more time learning about these and other terms as you progress.

There are other flight training requirements and FAA minimums to earn your certificate. The minimum flight time requirement to become a private pilot is 40 hours total. This includes at least 20 hours of dual flight training from an authorized instructor and 10 hours of solo flight time.

That's just a VERY basic overview of the 40 hours listed above. There are many areas of training and knowledge that must be gained such as night flying, cross country, test preparation, etc. The FAA lists every item required to be accomplished and you must meet all requirements before taking your checkride.

HOW LONG IS IT GOING TO TAKE?

Let me be real with you. Very few people complete their private pilot training near the FAA minimum of 40 hours. Some student pilots take twice as many hours to complete.

Realistically, the national average to earn a Private Pilot Certificate is somewhere between 65-70 flying hours. The term 'minimum' means just that – the least amount of hours required to apply to take a checkride. When calculating the time and money that it will cost you to complete, give yourself a range. No one is perfect and it may take you more than the minimum required time to understand each concept.

> **REAL WORLD TIP**
>
> This is getting a bit ahead of myself, but be aware that when going to a flight school to discuss prices for flight training, they may say... "Your certificate can cost you about $5,000!"
>
> Take note that those numbers might be based on the FAA minimum of 40 hours. This price may not reflect an accurate price because while it could be done in 40 hours, very few people complete their training near the FAA minimum.

I'm not saying that you can't complete your certificate in less than 50 hours. In fact, I have a great method that I'm going to share with you in this book that helps save time and money during your training. It is going to minimize many extra flight training hours off that bill, while maximizing your time spent on ground school and flight training. More on this later.

When it comes to ground school, MzeroA has developed a successful method over the years that will allow you to pass your FAA exams by spending two to three months, studying 3 days a week, for less than 2 hours each session using our proprietary Aviation Mastery Method. Some students need less time, others need a little longer but we are confident that you can find success with our online ground school.

Obtaining a Private Pilot Certificate is measured in proficiency and by standards established by the FAA. These standards can be found in a document called the Airman Certification Standards (ACS) which can be found on the FAA website (faa.gov). Every student should be familiar with these expectations prior to taking a checkride.

Generally, the more you fly and practice weekly, the shorter the journey may take. Said another way, one of the best ways to save time and money in your flight training is to increase the frequency of your flying and be consistent with it. You will realize during your flight training that the saying "time is money" is very true in aviation.

Typically, plan on flying at least once or twice per week to build your skill set. Life happens. Weather, combined with student, aircraft, and instructor availability often play a factor in the overall completion time. If you only schedule to fly once a week and have to cancel due to bad weather that day, then two weeks may go by before you can get back into the airplane. This often leads to the student having to review the last lesson and perhaps relearn a concept that has been forgotten due to the time gap. Not consistently moving forward in your training, slows down your progress, and also costs you more money in the long run.

IS FLYING SAFE?

Aviation is inherently the safest mode of transportation in the world. FAA regulations require that owners and operators maintain their aircraft in an "airworthy" or safe condition for flight. For example, aircraft used for flight instruction undergo two types of inspections: annual and every 100 flying hours.

Each year the aircraft must undergo a large maintenance check, called an annual inspection, where every inch of the aircraft is inspected to ensure airworthiness by a certificated airframe and power plant (A&P) mechanic with inspection authorization (IA). The 100 hour inspection is the same as the annual inspection, except it can be performed by any A&P mechanic. Completing the 100 hour inspection adds another layer of safety.

Along your journey, you'll learn how this rigorous maintenance compliance, combined with pilot proficiency and sound aeronautical decision making, influences the safety of flight. The more you learn about aviation, the safer you will feel flying because you will understand that airplanes just don't just fall out of the sky! As a pilot, we should strive to keep the most dangerous part of the flight, the drive to the airport. In fact, some pilots say they feel safer in their airplane rather than on the highway or in rush hour traffic.

WHERE DO I GET STARTED?

Maybe you are one of the lucky ones that have family or friends in aviation, or know someone that owns their own airplane and has taken you flying.

If you already know that you want to be a pilot, a great place to get started with your training is to enroll in a ground school. I recommend finding a ground school that offers courses that cater to your learning style, with accurate and relevant content. Most importantly, you want to make sure you are learning for the real-world, not just to pass the test with rote memorization techniques.

If you have never been in a small airplane before and you want to see if flying is for you, we will explain exactly what you need to do next to get you started.

According to the FAA, there are over 19,000 airports, heliports, seaplane bases, and other landing facilities in the United States and its territories. Included in those are over 3,000 general aviation (GA) airports, heliports and seaplane bases. General aviation airports are civilian (non-military) airports which do not have scheduled passenger airline service. Often, these smaller airports can be found close to your home and are easy to access.

These airports generally have one or more flight schools located on the field. Most flight schools offer something called a discovery flight, which allows you the opportunity to take a short flight with a qualified instructor, to get an idea if flying may be right for you.

Either call or visit the school and ask to schedule a discovery flight. Flying early in the morning or in the evening often provides cooler temperatures and smoother air conditions. You'll likely find that flying is much easier than you initially thought, and your first flight will be an experience you will never forget!

A discovery flight is led by a certificated flight instructor (CFI) with you flying in the left seat. That's right, you'll be in the pilot's seat! Don't worry though, the instructor can also control the aircraft from the other side. It may seem overwhelming at first, but by using a building block approach along with the MzeroA Aviation Mastery Method built into our Private Pilot Online Ground School, all the components will come together quicker than you probably imagined.

Discovery Flights tend to be relatively short, approximately 30 minutes total, just enough to get a feel for flying. You may get to taxi the airplane using your feet! Yes, steering the airplane on the ground is accomplished by using what is known as rudder pedals which are directly connected to a steerable nose wheel on the airplane. Rudder pedals are located near where the gas and brake pedals are in your car.

Once airborne, your instructor may demonstrate some maneuvers or encourage you to get the feel of flying the airplane by using the flight controls. At the end of flight, the instructor will perform the landing and may allow you to shadow the procedure by putting your hands lightly on the yoke which is somewhat similar to a steering wheel in a car.

After your discovery flight, take time to talk to your instructor about the experience. This is a good time to ask any questions you may have about the process. We'll talk more about choosing the right flight school and flight instructor in the next chapter.

HOW MUCH IS IT GOING TO COST?

The cost of flight training is going to vary widely. Many factors affect the total cost of learning how to fly and obtaining your pilot certificate. For example, the type of airplane you fly, how often you fly, and time it takes you to master the required skills needed to become a pilot, all play a part in total cost.

As mentioned earlier, the minimum amount of flight hours to become a private pilot is 40 hours but it can often take many more hours than that to complete the training. Aircraft are rented hourly, and time is tracked in 6-minute increments, or tenths of an hour. Aircraft rental costs range from about $100/hour all the way up to over $200/hour. Fuel is usually included in that cost, but not always. If fuel is not included, flight schools will refer to that as a "dry" rental price. Instructor fees are in addition to the aircraft rental and they may vary from location to location. These are questions you'll want to ask the flight school.

There's no getting around the fact that learning how to fly will be expensive. The bottom line is you can expect to invest between $7,000 to $10,000 or more, to complete your private pilot training. Of course this is an estimate and could vary widely depending on your location, and the overall amount of time it takes to build proficiency. That being said, there are several ways to save money during the flight training process and we'll discuss those in Chapter 2. Learning to fly an airplane is an attainable goal. If you think it may be for you, go give it a try. We bet you will love every minute!

Let me make one very clear point again. Two things will hold you back in your training: TIME and MONEY. "If you're concerned about finances during your training, I recommend starting a savings plan or budgeting an accurate amount to complete your training. Many student pilots make the mistake of budgeting just to complete solo, and find themselves running out of money in the middle of their training. Don't let this common mistake stop your dreams. I can assure you that with discipline and persistence a flight training budget can be successfully attained.

There are a few supplies that you will need to purchase along the way such as an aviation headset to use for communicating during flight, aeronautical charts for navigation, and a copy of your training aircraft's operating handbook. However, these are certainly not items that you need to purchase immediately. Later, we will discuss what items may be needed, and which are provided by your flight school.

CHAPTER 2
SET UP FOR SUCCESS

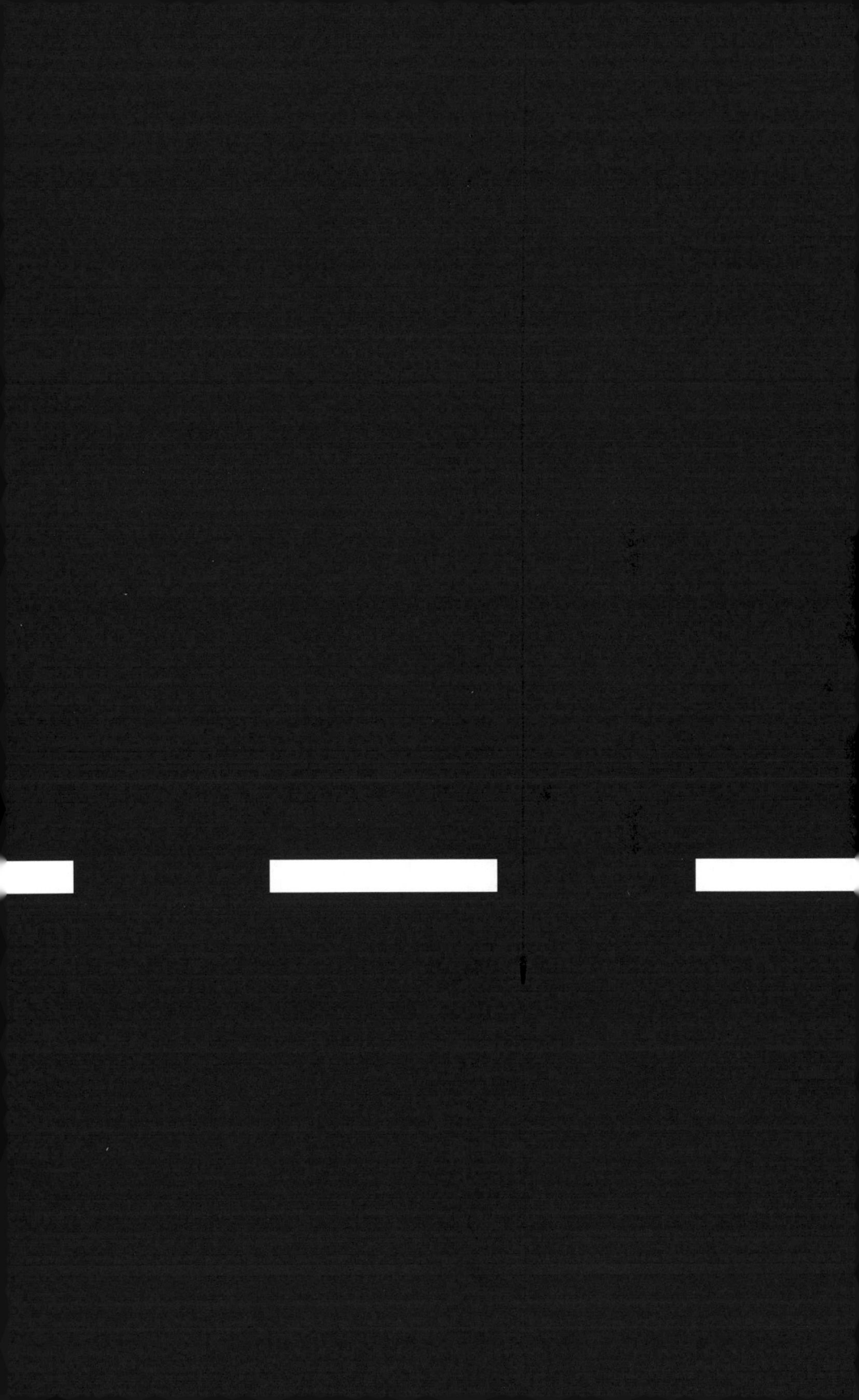

CHAPTER 2
Set up for Success

"You haven't seen a tree until you've seen its shadow from the sky."
-Amelia Earhart

Flight training requires significant time, dedication, and financial investment. However, there are ways to make your training more effective and efficient. There are two very important things that we're going to discuss: choosing the right flight school and the right flight instructor. Believe it or not, these two decisions can make or break your success in pilot training. A third part of this equation is choosing the right airplane in which to conduct your training.

Flight training can be done in accordance with either Part 61 or Part 141. This refers to the FAA rules and regulations regarding certification. We will discuss the difference between the two types and the advantages and disadvantages of flying at a part 61 versus part 141 flight school. We will address how they may influence your flight training and possibly future aviation career goals.

When selecting a flight school and instructor, it's a good idea When selecting a flight school and instructor, it's a good idea to approach it like a job interview; they must be the right fit for you. You need to realize that you will be spending thousands of dollars and many hours of your time at the flight school with your flight instructor. They should be working for your business, not the other way around—you are the employer and they are your employee. It's imperative that you feel comfortable and safe with the aircraft as well as have confidence in the instructor as you start your journey.

WHAT TO LOOK FOR IN A FLIGHT SCHOOL

When you start your search, it's important to make a list of multiple flight schools that you want to visit. Much like buying a car, you need to "test drive" more than one. You may want to take an introductory or discovery flight at multiple locations to see which school best fits your learning style.

Your overall first impression is very important in selecting a flight school. Consider your first impression of the aircraft.

What type of training aircraft does the school use? This will directly affect your budget. There are various types of general aviation aircraft. Some flight schools fly older aircraft with the classic round analog gauges while other flight schools operate newer glass panel style aircraft. Newer aircraft generally will cost more to rent but have newer technology. Perhaps your flight school only has newer Cessna 172s, while your budget aligns more with a Cessna 150. Trust me, this matters! When I started out I wanted to fly that beautiful brand new Cessna 172, but my wallet could only afford a 1962 Cherokee 140

REAL WORLD TIP

Find the trainer aircraft that fits your budget. Your private pilot certificate from the FAA is going to be the same regardless if you did your training with the new Cirrus SR22T or a 1962 Cherokee 140.

Federal regulations require that all training aircraft are maintained in an airworthy condition so it is more a matter of preference which aircraft you choose.

To be honest with you, I'm not a very handy person but when it comes to flying an airplane I'm quite selective. I look over all aircraft that I may potentially fly and consider them carefully. I advise that you do so as well. How do the training aircraft look at this flight school? You don't need to be a mechanic or particularly handy to see if the paint is chipping, if it has a moldy smell inside, corrosion, or bare aluminum visible to the naked eye. Most of the time the look and feel of the outside is directly related to the maintenance done in unseen places. Here is my personal theory: If the school can't clean up the bugs off the airplane, it may be a reflection of its care and maintenance in general.

Think about it this way, you are traveling and have paid a significant amount of money for a rental car. When you get there, the rental car company gives you a car that is dirty, dented, and smells awful. Would you take it or would you go right back to the desk and ask for another car? Why would your training aircraft be any different? If you see these signs, you can take a pretty good guess on what other corners have been cut on the real important stuff... like the engine!

Another good question to ask is: how many training aircraft does the school have in operation? Consider which aircraft the flight school offers. Ask if they have multiple aircraft and how many students and renter pilots they accommodate. If they have a high student to aircraft ratio, it may be difficult to fly when your schedule permits. If there is only one Cessna 152 and 20 students, it will be difficult to schedule the airplane during the time when you can fly. Also, what if the only airplane available goes down for maintenance? You can probably guess that your training will be interrupted!

It's important to ensure their availability fits with your schedule. Some flight schools have a standing schedule which means you always fly at the same time each week. If you can't get on the schedule often, it will increase the amount of time and money to complete your training. Consistently flying at least one to two times per week gives you a better chance to make continuous progress in your training.

Ask for a tour of their facility or maintenance shop and ask about their inspection process and procedures. Is the maintenance hangar clean and organized? Ask to see the aircraft maintenance logs. I even recommend asking to see how they keep track of the 100 hour and annual inspections. Do their aircraft logbooks look well-kept and up to date? Are they willing to show you the documents? If they seem unwilling, perhaps that's something to consider. Be mindful that some maintenance offices may be closed on the weekends and logbooks are usually kept there, in a safe, or other secure location. There may be a time where you can schedule to come back to view these as well. I know that this may sound like a lot but you will be flying and learning in this aircraft!

Consider the convenience of the training location. How far is the airport and flight school from your home or office? If you have to drive a far distance to get there, that could impact the amount of time you have available for flight training. At the same time, a good flight school is worth the drive! Is the flight school located at a busy airport? This may mean more time spent waiting for other aircraft to taxi, complete their takeoff or landing procedures, etc. but also gives you a great experience in a larger operating airport. So analyze your options wisely and choose what works best for you.

Ask the flight school if they have any discounts for a lump sum payment. In certain cases, schools may offer "block time discounts" for putting money into an account with them. For example, if you prepay for 10 flight hours, some flight schools may give 11 flight hours credit for advance payment. Be sure the flight school maintains a great business reputation before putting that amount of money down! Perhaps even try a few flight lessons with them and make sure they are a good fit for you before putting a lot of money into an account with the flight school. Again, this "block time" purchase is generally not required, but instead an opportunity to save some money.

Does the flight school have a structured training plan, known as a syllabus? This is one of the most important pieces to help keep your training on track. A syllabus sets the objectives and lets you know exactly what will be covered in each lesson, and the standards and metrics to which you are measured. It allows you to review and study before each lesson and gives your instructor a place to make notes during the lesson for a debrief. A syllabus also allows you to easily view your progress. You aren't just flying for the sake of it; you are working towards earning your pilot certificate. A syllabus is a scripted and measured approach which generally works better when on your journey to become a pilot

I can't emphasize enough the importance of following a syllabus. When I was working on my commercial pilot certificate during an airline hiring boom, I had 8 different CFIs because they kept leaving to fly for the airlines. During that period, we did not follow a syllabus and I transitioned to 8 different opinions, 8 different voices... My first CFI knew I was great at steep turns but had a fear of stalls at the time. That knowledge never got communicated over to the second CFI in the same flight school. So what did the second CFI do? We had to fly a few times just to go over all different maneuvers so the new CFI could get an idea of where I was in my training. Now, imagine this situation with 8 different CFIs...I was very frustrated to say the least! Not having every flight lesson documented cost me a lot of time and money because we didn't have a syllabus with notes and progress reports. If my flying would have been documented well, the next CFI that I was assigned would have been able to see it and move forward accordingly. This is why it is so important to make sure, no matter if you fly at a mom-and-pop flight school or a large "chain" flight school, that you use and follow a syllabus.

Another way to save money on your flight training is to complete some of your training in a flight simulator. Be sure to investigate if the flight school owns or has access to an aviation training device (ATD) referred to as a simulator. Training time in an approved ATD can account for part of your total flight training curriculum and is very beneficial for learning procedures, often at a fraction of the cost of the actual aircraft rental.

The right ground school training is perhaps one of the most critical parts of your training. Your ground school not only saves you time and money on earning your certificate, but it also forms your foundation in aeronautical concepts and emergency procedures for safe, real-world flying. As we discussed, you will need to pass an FAA exam that tests your aeronautical knowledge of aerodynamics, weather, performance, systems, regulations, and more. Many learners don't realize that examiners note the areas of deficiency on the knowledge test. Your score from the knowledge test and the areas that were incorrect are one of the first things that most FAA examiners notice.

At the end of your FAA knowledge test results page any incorrect answers are coded according to the associated area of knowledge that you missed. The FAA examiner will typically start asking questions and testing your knowledge on those areas that were found to be deficient on the knowledge test. In order for our students to master and troubleshoot their areas of deficiency, we have developed a tool for MzeroA Online Ground School members. Learners can input their incorrect answer codes from their knowledge test, and our system will develop specific quizzes and practice tests from just these incorrect areas to fine tune your knowledge. You can continue learning after passing the knowledge test and become even more prepared for your checkride! This is truly what we stand for, **A GOOD PILOT IS ALWAYS LEARNING.** It's not a slogan, it is truly our mission to learn beyond the FAA tests. MzeroA has everything you need to not only pass the knowledge test and have a strong base of knowledge to take into the air for the flying portion of training, but most importantly become a safe-real world pilot. Hundreds of thousands of students have found success by using MzeroA courses.

PART 61 VERSUS PART 141

When choosing a flight school, you'll hear about two options when it comes to selecting a flight school: Part 61 and Part 141. The "Part" refers to the applicable section in Title 14 of the Code of Federal Regulations that specifies the required flight and ground experience required to become a pilot. We often abbreviate this as 14 CFR or 41 and just use the word "Part" so if you want to look up the specific regulation, you can search for "14 CFR Part 61" or "14 CFR Part 141." While the legal language used in the regulations can be confusing for a prospective pilot candidate, we're going to explain the differences in plain English so you know which one is the right one for you. While both types of flight instruction are legitimate methods of pilot training, there are pros and cons of each and it is important to choose the best option for you.

PART 61 describes the certification of pilots, flight, and ground instructors. It establishes eligibility, aeronautical knowledge, and minimum flight time requirements to obtain various pilot certifications. The Part 61 training environment is less regimented than Part 141 and leaves an instructor with more flexibility to adjust the training program as needed for student success. While Part 141 certainly offers a structured path to success, it's essential to consider the unique advantages and challenges of Part 61 flight training.

1. Flexible Scheduling: Part 61 provides flexibility in scheduling, but this can sometimes result in longer gaps between training sessions, potentially causing regression in skills and leading to additional time and financial investment.
2. Tailored to Full-Time Commitments: Part 61 training is designed primarily for individuals who are working or have other commitments that limit their ability to engage in full-time flight training. This approach enables student pilots to balance their flight training with everyday life.

3. Consideration for Future Employers: It's worth noting that employers will hire both Part 141 and Part 61 training backgrounds, and while Part 61 is a valid training path, some aviation employers may prefer candidates with Part 141 training due to its structured and standardized nature.

PART 141 uses a more regimented certification process. The syllabus has a structured lesson plan and it includes specific areas of knowledge that must be included. A Part 141 pilot school must seek and maintain FAA approval for its training curriculum, syllabus, and lesson plans. They must also maintain a satisfactory pass rate for their program. While different in the process, both training programs teach to the same FAA certification standards.

1. Structured Success: Part 141 schools offer a well-structured curriculum, guaranteeing that you'll receive comprehensive training that meets the highest industry standards.
2. FAA Seal of Approval: These schools are regularly evaluated by the FAA, assuring you that your training will consistently adhere to rigorous regulatory standards.
3. Preferred by Future Employers: Many aviation employers hold Part 141 training in high regard due to its comprehensive and standardized approach.

One main advantage to training with a Part 141 flight school is that students can progress quickly through their training. Since the Part 141 curriculum has stringent 42 oversight and regulation by the FAA, students can gain certification with fewer flight hours. For example, a Private Pilot Certificate requires a minimum of 35 flight hours of flight experience under Part 141 versus 40 hours under Part 61. The ground training requirements are also different. Part 141 requires a minimum of 35 hours of approved ground school training, while Part 61 has no minimum requirement. Remember, ground school is critical to building your knowledge, which makes your flight time far more effective. Regardless of whether you are training part 141 or part 61, taking the time to learn and gain a good foundation of aeronautical knowledge on the ground allows you to focus on flying skills in the air.

The training time differences are greater for advanced certificates and ratings. For example, the commercial pilot certificate can be accomplished in just 190 flight hours under Part 141, as opposed to 250 hours under Part 61. However, certain Part 141 flight schools have the FAA approval to offer an abbreviated commercial course, approximately 50 hours. Keep in mind that all the times mentioned are the minimum hours, not necessarily how many it will take you to complete the course.

If you plan to move or relocate to a different flight school during flight training, there are some additional considerations. One potential disadvantage of part 141 training is it can be difficult to transfer training time from a Part 61 school to a Part 141 school or even between two different Part 141 schools.

The FAA permits Part 141 schools to give credit for not more than 25% of the curriculum requirement for 43 knowledge and experience from a Part 61 school. The FAA also only allows up to 50% credit to be received between Part 141 schools. So, if moving may be on your horizon, it may be worth it to talk with your instructor to find out which program best suits your needs. The best way to avoid losing any credit is to complete a certificate or rating before switching flight schools if possible.

Ultimately, the decision between Part 141 and Part 61 depends on your individual goals and learning style. Both paths offer unique advantages, and the key is to select the one that resonates most with your aspirations. Part 141 provides structured excellence, while Part 61 offers flexibility – choose the path that best suits your journey towards a fulfilling aviation career.

CHOOSING A FLIGHT INSTRUCTOR

Choosing the right flight instructor is crucial to your success. You will be learning from your flight instructor all along the way while sharing close quarters in the airplane. Being able to trust and feel comfortable with your instructor creates a good environment for learning and mentorship. It is important that this person is invested in you and your success. You will spend many hours together, so choose someone that you get along with and respect. Look for an instructor that strives to stay current with the industry changes, and continues to grow and improve their own knowledge. I always say that your learning will mirror the level of expertise of your CFI! If your CFI's weakness is in following a checklist or crosswind landings, guess where your weakness is probably going to be? You also want to choose an instructor who matches your learning style.

What is your learning style? This may be a question you've never asked yourself or thought about in the past. However, it is quite relevant as learning will be more effective and efficient if your instructor can deliver information in a method that you can best receive, process, understand, and ultimately apply.

Do you learn best by reading and then later recalling that information? Are you a visual learner where pictures and graphs help you process the information? Are you a combination of both? Do you need time to absorb information and process it? All of these learning methods can be tailored to you by a well-qualified and adaptable instructor to best suit your learning needs. Knowing how you best learn information and expressing that to your CFI will help the process.

What happens if you don't mesh with your prospective or current instructor and some conflict occurs along the way? Learning a new skill is challenging, which can be compounded by being in a confined space. It is okay to request a change of instructor. It's not a personal thing and happens on occasion. In fact, I recommend flying with another instructor if, at some point during your training, you feel you are hitting a plateau. Second opinions can be really helpful! The school's responsibility is to help you achieve your dream with a safe and successful outcome. A good flight school will be more than happy to accommodate you with another instructor; don't be afraid to ask.

Take the time to do the research and remember you are hiring the instructor and have the power to vote with your dollars. Make sure you find a CFI that you truly mesh with and never forget that you are paying them for their services.

I was very young when I started my private pilot training and throughout my career, I have had all types of instructors. Some were very encouraging and excellent teachers while other instructors clearly did not have passion for teaching. One even suggested that I give up my dream and told me "Jason, maybe you are not meant to fly." GREAT instructors make every minute count. Now, being a CFII and with the experience I gained with more than 15 years of being in the industry, I've created what I call the "MzeroA CFI Interview" with the questions I wish someone would have told me to ask when choosing a flight instructor. The questions include:

- What is the CFI's schedule? Is the CFI full time with the flight school and available every day, or is he/she only available on the weekends? Make sure your schedules match. If you are available during a weekday, you would not be a good candidate for an instructor who can ONLY fly weekends.

- What are your CFI's goals and career aspirations? I mentioned earlier my experience in changing CFIs 8 times because they were moving onto working for the airlines and I had to retrace my training for each new instructor. If I had known that they were about to leave, I would have continued my search for someone who was dedicated to instructing. It is very frustrating when your CFI leaves to pursue her/his dreams and you get stuck with someone who knows NOTHING about you or your training progress. While that is great for them, it may not be the best for your training journey unless you document your progress thoroughly.

- How many students does the prospective instructor have on his/her schedule? My recommendation is to find someone with less than eight students since eight is the maximum number of students a full time instructor can handle at any one time. Cut this number in half for a part time CFI. These numbers are my opinion based on experience as both a student and CFI. You don't want to get lost in the shuffle and have future scheduling issues, so avoid this early on your journey of choosing a flight instructor.

- What is your Pass Rate? Here is a question NO CFI should hesitate to answer. If an instructor has a pass rate under 80%, that means that the FAA will probably be investigating such a low pass rate with this instructor or flight school and possibly recommend recurrent training for them. Knowing that below 80% is a red flag for unsatisfactory instruction, you should make sure you get this question answered. Also, please keep in mind your CFI may be new and hasn't yet recommended anyone for a checkride. Being their first student is not necessarily a bad sign. Most new CFIs have not had time to develop bad habits and are fresh from doing their own training!

- What's their reputation? With the power of the internet you will have no problem finding reviews or information online. Even asking around the airport and finding recurrent students of your prospective CFI. Additionally, a good CFI will provide references from past students for you to contact. Realize that you will be spending many hours with this person and in a very small space. Please take the time to learn more about the person, make sure he/she will be a good influence, mentor and make smart decisions in your training.

- Is the flight instructor responsible and dedicated? The CFI is responsible for teaching you to be a safe pilot and make smart decisions to be able to take family and friends flying to beautiful places. It's a tremendous responsibility for the instructor to ensure they impart a great amount of knowledge, experience, and skill to you. Thus, the instructor should be held accountable for the quality of teaching given to their students. You want a CFI that is passionate about always learning and teaching. Someone who can be a good influence on you, help you make smart decisions and will take the time to come prepared for your flight lessons. They should also point out additional resources to make your dream of becoming a private pilot a reality. There are outstanding flight instructors out there, passionate about aviation and born to teach!

HOW DO I SELECT AN AIRPLANE?

What airplane is right for you and how do you know? Choosing the right airplane for you can be daunting. There are two main types of aircraft: high-wing, with the wing above you, and low-wing, with the wing below you.

If the flight school has both types, try sitting in both and look outside from the pilot's seat. Is one more comfortable for you? Does one offer better visibility?

Another driver for airplane selection is cost. If the flight school has a wide range of aircraft, perhaps the older models may be better for your budget. Newer aircraft, with advanced avionics and sophisticated technology, generally carry a higher price tag per hour. Flying an older model airplane may lower the overall cost, then perhaps you can move up to a new airplane later in your journey. When you take your checkride, you'll need to know how to operate all the systems in the airplane in which you are testing. Having systems that are simple and less advanced may be easier to manage. Some pilots prefer more automation and technology. Talk to your instructor about what might work best for you.

OUR AVIATION COMMUNITY

You are not alone in making this decision. Pilots like to hang out at airports. Spend time talking to them on your visit to the airport, and listen to the vast array of opinions. Their experiences with the flight school are a great indicator if you will be happy there. Often listening to other pilots' experiences, called "hanger talk", is also a great learning tool.

The MzeroA Nation comprises thousands of learners, successful pilots, and instructors at all levels, all of whom have been in your position and are eager to help others. This is the most generous group of people that I have ever met, they go above and beyond to help others pursue their aviation dreams and share the love for flying. The moment they learn that you share the same passion and love for aviation, you will be embraced. They treat each other as family, thus we refer to them as the MzeroA family! You can find the group by searching "MzeroA

Nation" on Facebook. We also meet every week on webinars in the MzeroA Online Ground School. Join the group to find fellow aviation enthusiasts. You will find many experienced, knowledgeable and fun people who truly are more of an aviation family than a group. Eventually, you'll find yourself helping new students coming into aviation behind you!

CHAPTER 3
GETTING STARTED

CHAPTER 3
Getting Started

"If birds can glide for long periods of time, why can't I?"
-Orville Wright

One of the best ways to save time and money in your flight training is to complete your ground school first. I've often said that my dream student is one who comes to me with a medical in hand, a written test done, and ready to start flying. Having served over 130,000 pilots, myself and the MzeroA team see the data each day backing up the fact that doing your ground school first is the single greatest factor in saving money. In the same way we recommend you to go learn more about your flight school and your CFI before you spend any money with them, we believe you should have the same opportunity to check out the online ground school first before spending any money. This is why we offer two week FREE trial.

IMPORTANCE OF GROUND SCHOOL

Every pilot should aim to build a foundation of knowledge that is applicable in real-world scenarios. What do I mean by that? I believe that knowledge is not power, it is only potential power unless you know how to apply it! Some ground schools focus on helping you pass the FAA knowledge test through rote memorization alone. In other words, they will literally instruct you to memorize the questions and answers to just pass the test. While this may sound good to some, what happens if you are at 5,000 feet traveling at 90 knots and you need to apply an emergency procedure? Oh... that was answer C on the test...but now what? Unfortunately, I'm serious that this is real and does happen. That's why it is crucial to find a ground school that teaches you real-world applicability in a way that simplifies the complex concepts, so you can see why to do it, how to do it, when to do it and most importantly understand it! Just rote memorization alone will cost you long term.

We have seen many students spending more time and money in their ground school than needed because they don't take it seriously. Initially, they believe it is enough to just purchase test prep software or books to memorize questions and answers to pass the knowledge test. Often, it isn't until later in their training or during checkride preparations that students realize they can't apply what they've memorized, or worse, they've forgotten the procedures altogether. Then, they go buy the MzeroA ground school that focuses not only on passing the FAA exams, but most importantly how to learn and understand the concepts. You will learn how and when to apply them in the airplane so you become a safe-real world pilot.

In the interest of safety, the FAA has moved to more scenario based examinations. They also don't want you simply memorizing information without knowing how to apply it. Checkride examiners continually tell us how they now conduct scenario-based checkrides and less than prepared applicants struggle. Possessing the knowledge and giving direct answers to examiner questions showcases your proficiency.

Building a strong foundation with accurate information and real-world applicability is crucial, not only to pass your test but also to potentially save your life. I'm a true believer that what you learn first is the most lasting. In the case of an emergency you will always fall back to your foundation. This is why we developed the MzeroA Aviation Mastery Method, which has helped over 130,000 pilots earn their certificates. Our instruction is based on the science of learning, aiming to create a rock-solid mindset both in the air and on the ground.. Our members consistently achieve higher scores on their FAA exams than the national average. We are so confident in our training method that we offer a guarantee that you'll pass your test.*

If you are serious about your training and seek relevant and accurate information, MzeroA is your go-to learning resource. Our easy-to-understand online courses are designed to create safer, smarter pilots. We believe that "A Good Pilot Is Always Learning" and have built that mantra into our teaching methods, that is why our courses and resources are frequently updated and improved. The Aviation Mastery Method strives to teach in an easy-to-understand way and offers different ways of learning the aviation concepts for different learning styles. We're in the business of building safe real-world pilots.

*See mzeroa.com website for our terms and conditions.

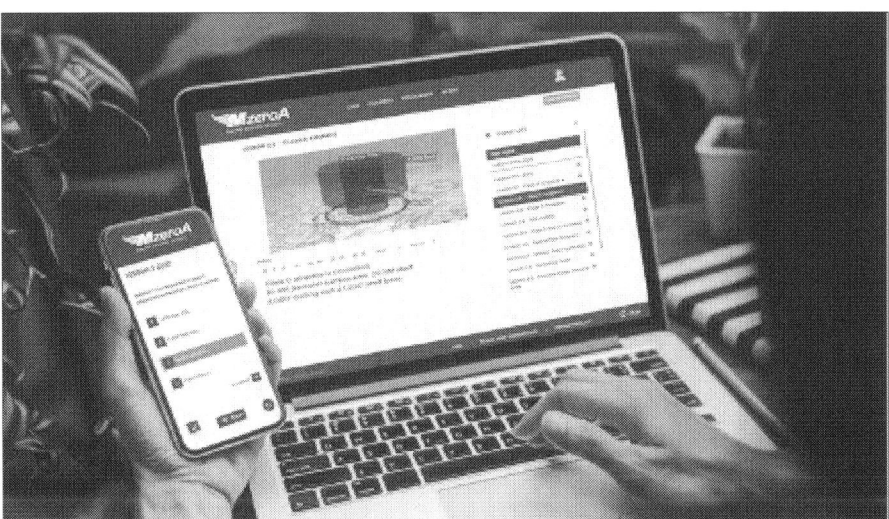

When selecting your ground school, visit MzeroA.com and check out the Aviation Mastery Method. We'll talk about this more along the way but if you are ready now and excited to begin, you can start your training with us today!

WHAT ELSE DO I NEED?

To pass the FAA test, you have all you need inside the MzeroA Online Ground School. As far as books go, the MUST HAVE BOOKS are the FAR/AIM, Airman Certification Standards, Airplane Flying Handbook and The Pilot's Handbook of Aeronautical Knowledge (PHAK). If you are a type of person that likes to have printed paper copies, you can get these books online or in most pilot shops located at local airports. But please make sure you are buying the latest and most current version, the FAR/AIM updates every year so get the current year version. If you prefer digital copies, you can download the documents or e-books for free directly from the FAA website. I personally get the digital copies on my computer and tablet since the FAA can release a new version of most of these every year, so I don't have to buy new books constantly. If you need help to understand what the FAR/AIM is saying and how to apply the FAA regulations, we have dedicated videos inside the MzeroA Online Ground School specific just for that subject.

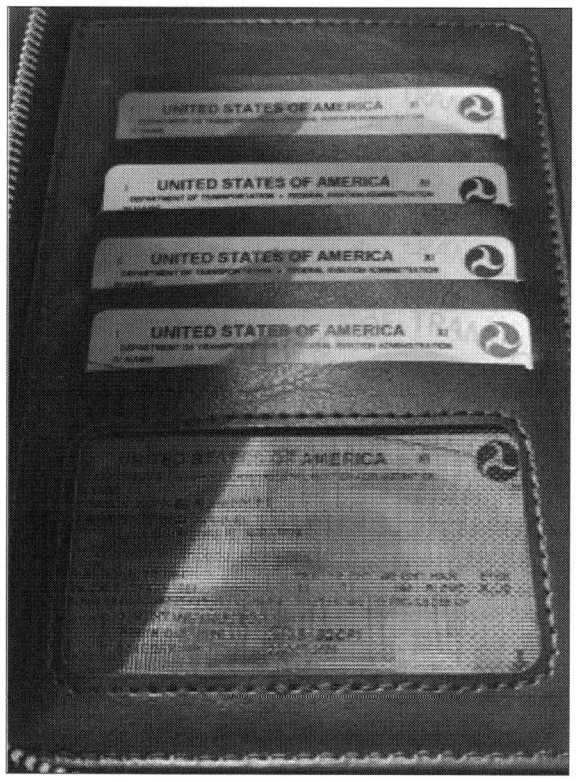

There are two more important documents you will need once you get started with your flight training: a student pilot certificate and an FAA medical certificate. These aren't needed on day one of flight training, but as mentioned earlier, we can't encourage you enough to get these as soon as possible since they will be needed relatively soon after you begin training.

You will need a student pilot certificate from the FAA to conduct solo flights, a required part of your training. You and your flight instructor will work through the process together and fill out the paperwork online. Several weeks later, your student pilot certificate will be mailed to you from the FAA.

As mentioned in Chapter 1, a FAA-issued Medical Certificate is required. It is a routine physical examination conducted by an AME who is a certified aviation physician. There are three classifications of medical certificates: Class I, Class II and Class III. The requirement and duration of them is based on each class and is set forth in 14 CFR 61.23. The criteria required to pass the medical exam are set forth in 14 CFR Part 67. For student pilot or private pilot privileges, a Class III is required. To find an AME near you, the FAA has a searchable AME locator tool available online. If you plan to fly as a profession, consider getting a first Class medical to ensure that you can attain it because it will be required. "This class of medical certificate has the most stringent standards, so it is advantageous to determine early in your training whether you meet these requirements. Regardless of which class of medical you decide to get, be sure to complete this step well before stepping into an airplane. Remember, this can help save you time and money! Ensuring that you can hold a medical and completing the process before flight training sets you up for success.

If you're a U.S. Citizen, getting started is a relatively easy process. You'll need to provide proof of citizenship prior to starting any flight training. Examples of these can be a birth certificate, a valid and unexpired U.S. Passport, an original United States naturalization certificate with raised seal, or a Certificate of Naturalization issued by the U.S. Citizenship and Immigration Services (USCIS) or the U.S. Immigration and Naturalization Service (INS).

If you're a non-U.S. Citizen, or non-U.S. National there are some additional steps needed to begin flying. The Flight Training Security Program (FTSP) is a process, where documents are uploaded to the Transportation Security Administration (TSA) database for approval. Student fingerprints must be taken and submitted to the TSA. Once those documents are approved, and a few additional steps are taken, flight training can commence after the flight school receives TSA approval. If this situation applies to you, visit the TSA Flight Training Security Program online for more information (fts.tsa. dhs.gov). A good flight school will help you with this process so don't worry!

You're about to get your first and important piece of equipment needed when learning to fly – your logbook. Your pilot logbook holds your flight history and record.

It is where you will document your flying and training as well as the place where you will be endorsed and authorized for certain flying activities. You can purchase a logbook from a pilot shop or online, and many pilots maintain both digital and paper versions. Take time to select the one you like; it will be with you forever.

REAL WORLD TIP

Make sure your logbook is legible and accurate. Always record flight hours in black or blue pen. Many pilots also use a digital logbook or scan copies of completed pages as a backup source and keep the logbook in a fireproof safe. This is your record of flight training and a very important document that you will keep forever.

Pilots tend to love gadgets and technology and you'll probably hear about all the latest trends when you're hanging around the airport. There are certain items that you'll need but aren't necessary on the first day.

Items such as a headset, flight computer, aeronautical charts, and a flight bag to store all this gear can all come later. A headset is a very important part of flight training because that's how you communicate in the airplane. Your headset will also protect your hearing so it's important that you try on different styles and brands to find one that's comfortable for you. Typically, they can cost from a few hundred dollars to well over $1,000. You'll be wearing the headset every time you fly, so consider this when making your purchase. Your instructor and other pilot reviews can all add valuable input on your purchase. These are just some basics! You don't need to run out today and get all this stuff, buy it as you need it. Some flight schools will also let you borrow these items.

At this stage, you should have discussed your training plan with your instructor and completed the necessary paperwork. Now is the time to get that ground school training done so that you can successfully move into the airplane with a strong base of knowledge.

CHAPTER 4
THE JOURNEY

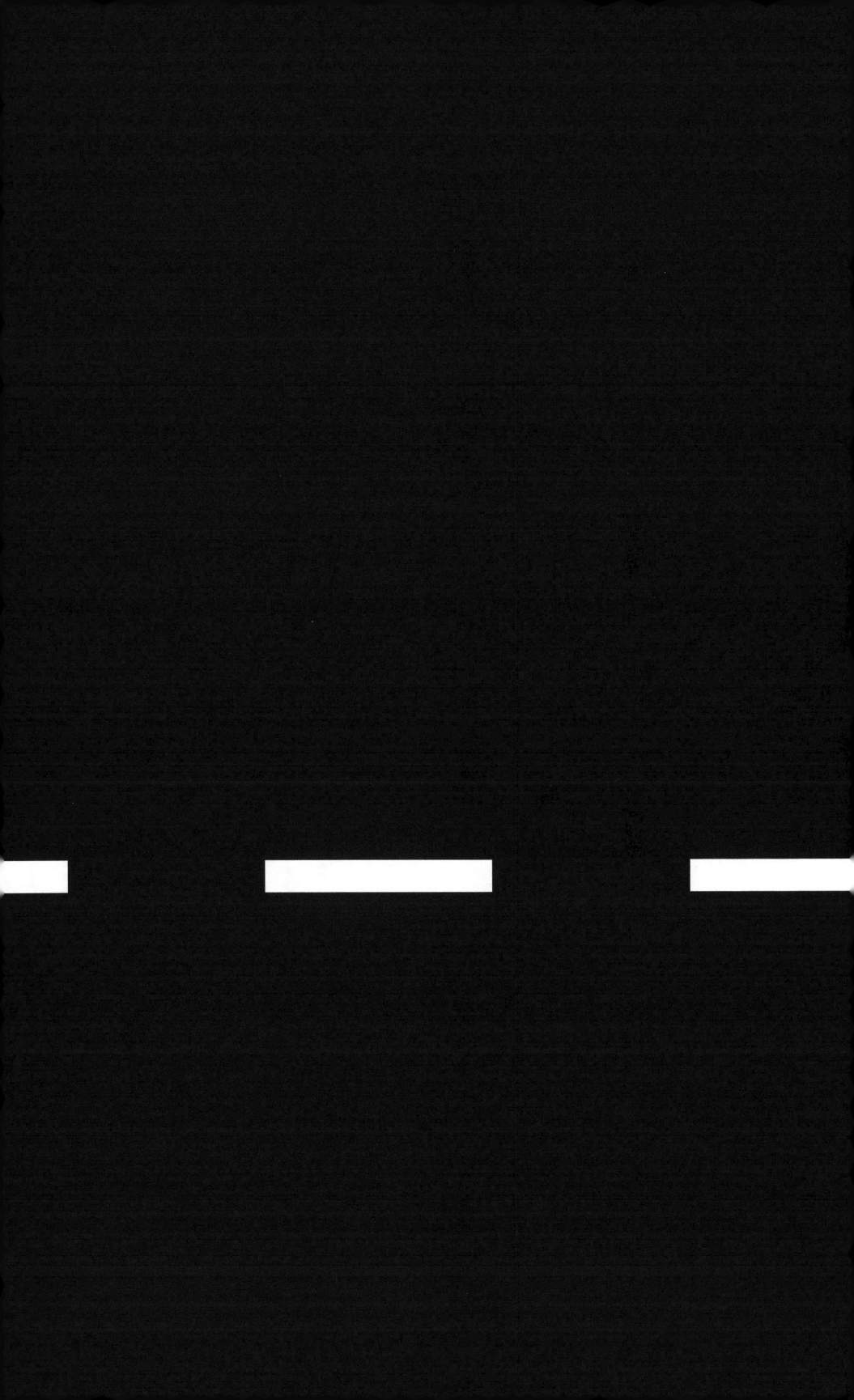

CHAPTER 4
The Journey

"To be absolutely alone for the first time in the cockpit of a plane hundreds of feet above the ground is an experience never to be forgotten."

-Charles Lindbergh

As the pieces come together, let's delve deeper into the flight training process. Keep in mind that this journey is how you will learn and grow to become a good pilot, enjoy the process!

LAYING THE GROUNDWORK

There is much to learn about flying and aviation in general. From aerodynamics and weather, to airport operations and regulations, it can all seem overwhelming. That's why MzeroA is here, to make your dream and goal of becoming a pilot more attainable. A key difference from other courses, aside from our quality customer support, is that MzeroA uses a building block approach, known as the Aviation Mastery Method. Our ground school programs break down material into smaller, more manageable parts, building on what you know and expanding that knowledge to become a safer pilot. We can't state enough that a good pilot is always learning and our ground school will prove to be invaluable on your journey. The online ground school is set up strategically in a way that when you are learning a particular topic or maneuver, you can reinforce the knowledge thoroughly. You can find more information on the Aviation Mastery Method and available courses at the end of this book.

We emphasize the importance of ground school due to the substantial value it adds to your training. It offers an opportunity to go back and watch any lessons and topics over and over until you understand them. You can also work with your instructor on the ground and create a stationary, or static environment where you and your instructor can sit in the airplane and learn to use the avionics in the airplane without the added task of flying. We often say the airplane is a terrible classroom; it's loud, fast, and there is no pause button. Learning to tune the radios, or spending time in the maintenance shop learning about the engine from mechanics, can provide significant benefits along the way. The more you learn on the ground translates to more effective use of time in the air, and that can save you thousands of dollars over the course of your training.

Additionally, your instructor should be making time for both pre-flight and post-flight briefings. This should be mandatory and is crucial to your flight training! I'm seeing more and more instructors just walking away from a lesson, not even giving their students a "Great job with your landings today!" as feedback. Instead, they quickly make their way back to the front desk to meet with the next student. Conducting a brief before and after your flight lesson is another great way to save time and money on your training.

A pre-flight briefing covers all pertinent details for that day's flight. Before each flight, you and your instructor should have a pre-flight briefing. At first, your instructor will lead the pre-brief and teach you how to check the current weather for the flight, flight restrictions, and potential risks for flight. You will also go over the weight and balance of aircraft and performance data for your flight. As you become more familiar with how to gather this information, you as the student, will be expected to lead the briefing. Both the instructor and student should verify that they have all needed documents and are in a "fit condition" to fly. This means both you and your instructor feel physically and mentally prepared to fly. I'm getting ahead of myself here but the FAA has a great health assessment to use before each flight, you will learn more about this in the online ground school. After those items are completed, your instructor should clearly state the objective for the flight that you are about to conduct. It is also a smart idea for you to review the syllabus and what the flight lesson will include prior to arriving. Every student should come prepared for a flight lesson. This will also save you time and money because you will be ready and not waste flight time going over information that you could have reviewed on the ground or at home.

Immediately after your flight lesson, a post-flight briefing should be accomplished. "This session allows both of you to discuss successful maneuvers and identify areas for improvement. The post-flight briefing takes a bit longer but it's also where you can get the most valuable feedback and understanding of areas of improvement from the day's lesson. It is a recap infused with constructive criticism. You can create a plan of action and steps towards reaching the required performance in the future.

Early in my instructing years, I noticed that when I gave students instant feedback while flying, they acknowledged it by saying "yes" to everything. When I brought the same thing up on the ground they would say things like "Oh yes, that makes sense!" as if it was the first time they had even heard it. This is another example of how the airplane can be a terrible classroom. While I still gave feedback while flying, I made sure to mention it again after the flight because there is so much going on during the flight that makes the knowledge retention rate for new student pilots very low.

> **REAL WORLD TIP**
>
> Don't be afraid to ask your instructor questions! If there is something you don't understand or it doesn't make sense to you, question it. You won't sound stupid. In fact, learners that ask questions are interested in gaining a deeper understanding. Even ask another instructor if you feel the need to do so. If you just can't grasp a certain concept, sometimes the way another instructor explains it will click with you better.

Don't underestimate the value of pre-flight and post-flight time. They are an important aspect to your training.

HOW AIRPLANES FLY

There's a long-standing joke "What makes an airplane fly?" and the response often is "Money!" While that is partly true, let's discuss the physics of what makes an airplane actually fly. The answer is aerodynamics and lift. Understanding the science behind flight can help ease some student pilot's nerves as they begin training.

Aircraft are exposed to the four forces of flight:

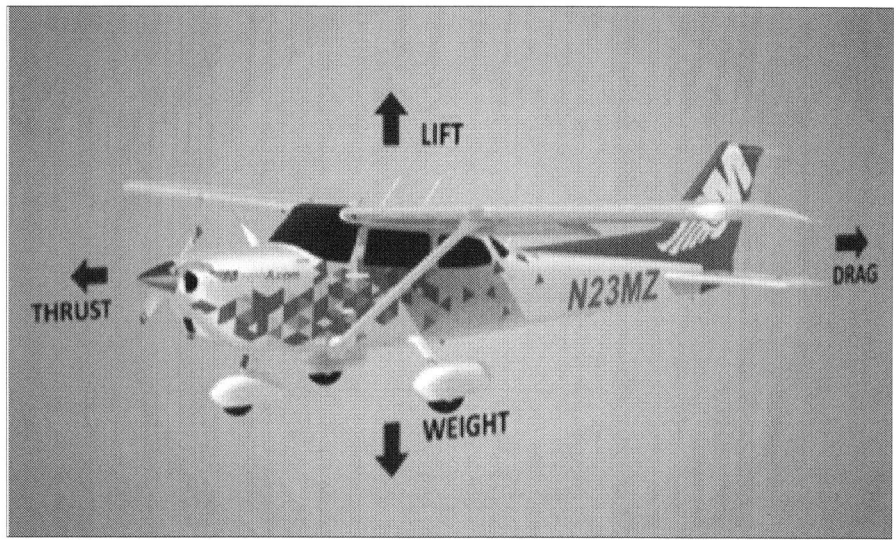

- Lift (upward force generated by airflow over and under the wings)
- Weight (downward force of aircraft due to gravity)
- Thrust (forward force provided by the powerplant/ and propeller)
- Drag (rearward force created as the airplane moves through the air)

While wings create lift to keep an airplane in the air, these four forces are behind how that is possible. Pilots learn how the forces work and how to control them with flight controls and power.

As the figure above illustrates, the four forces acting on the airplane allows the aircraft to maneuver. Each force has an opposite force that works against it. Lift acts in the opposite direction to weight, supporting the plane against gravity. Thrust works against drag. When the forces are balanced, the aircraft is in equilibrium. Generally speaking, the aircraft climbs if the forces of lift and thrust are greater than gravity and drag. However, if gravity and drag are greater than lift and thrust, the airplane descends.

The specific shape of the wing, designed to generate lift, is called an airfoil. If you look at the cross section of most wings, you'll see a curved surface on the top with more of a straight surface on the bottom. This shape creates the aerodynamics of lift in flight when the air flows around the wing surfaces. Part of the air flow moves above the wing, and part of it flows beneath the wing. The curved shape on the top portion of the wing causes the air to travel faster creating a low pressure area. The opposite is true on the bottom section of the wing. Airflow moves slower creating a higher pressure area. The result is lift. This concept is based on Bernoulli's Principle of Pressure dating back to the 1700's!

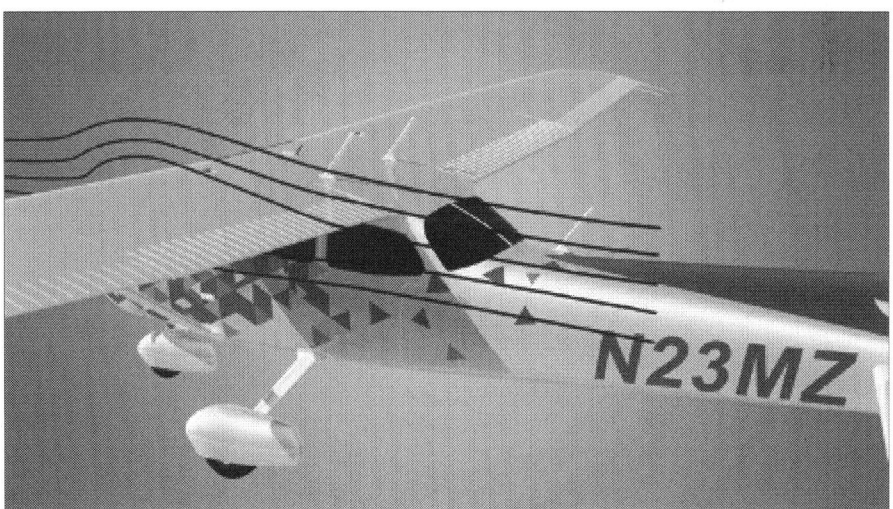

STAGES OF FLIGHT TRAINING

This chapter will probably make a lot more sense to someone who has at least taken a ground school or a few lessons. So if this chapter is hard for you to follow, don't worry, you will get there. I encourage you to use the link provided earlier to access the online ground school to get better visuals.

The flight training process can be divided into four distinct stages:

1. Pre-solo maneuvers
2. Your first solo
3. Cross country planning
4. Solo cross country

PRE-SOLO MANEUVERS

I'm a big advocate of helping student pilots understand WHY we do each maneuver. Very early on in my training I had no idea why certain maneuvers were required. My instructor would instruct me to 'do this maneuver,' and I would comply without understanding why.

In your first few hours of flight training, you will practice many procedures, such as ground operations and taxiing the aircraft. You'll learn proper taxi technique and how to navigate the airport paying attention to runway signs and markings. You'll work through preflight checks of the aircraft and systems before take off from the airport.

Once airborne, you'll spend time learning about how those four forces of flight impact the airplane and how they all interact. Your instructor may point out and demonstrate ground reference maneuvers, showing your ground track, or path along the ground to show you the importance of wind and its effects on the aircraft. You'll learn how to smoothly fly the airplane, often with your fingertips, or a very light grip, instead of the common misperception that you should have a "death grip" on the controls.

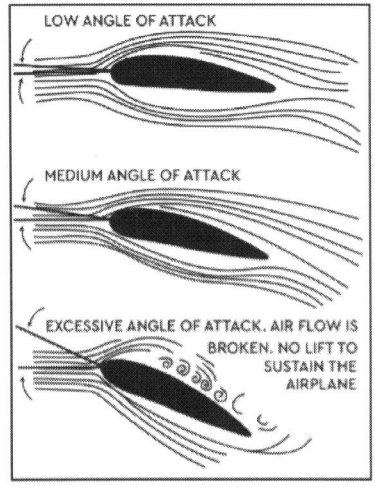

As you continue your lessons in the pre-solo phase, you'll be introduced to maneuvers such as steep turns, slow flight, and stalls. Now, let's tackle some misconceptions about stalls!

Stalls are a significant safety concern during flight because they disrupt the airflow over the wings. There are different types of stalls but for the sake of this short introduction, we will refer to aerodynamic stalls not engine stalls. This occurs when there simply is not enough airflow to move over the wing and that smooth layer of air that flows over the wing is interrupted. It has absolutely nothing to do with the engine quitting or any other misnomers. Why do we practice stalls? So, we can recognize the flight characteristics that cause stalls and build proficiency in both avoiding and recovering from them. Simply said, we practice stalls to practice recoveries. Perhaps you accidentally pitched too steeply on takeoff or got a little too slow on final approach to landing. Knowing how to recover from mishaps that may lead to a stall is crucial for safety. It's important to practice these at altitudes high enough to allow sufficient time to recover.

Most checkride examiners are less concerned with how you get into the stall, they want to see how efficiently you recover. In the online ground school you will learn about all types of stalls.

Steep turns are a performance maneuver where the pilot simultaneously maintains a constant altitude and 45- degree bank angle in the aircraft. This maneuver could be used if two aircraft are converging head-on, to avoid an obstacle, or whenever a quick turn is necessary. There are standards set for the maneuver and when proficient in the maneuver, you'll be able to hold altitude within + or − 100 ft while completing a 360-degree turn in either direction. This means if your flight instructor instructs you to maintain an altitude of 3,500 feet, you should stay within 100 feet of this level, not dropping below 3,400 or rising above 3,600 feet.

Slow flight is as straightforward as it sounds. I'm a big advocate of practicing slow flight on a regular basis. In fact, I believe you cannot be truly great at landings until you've mastered slow flight. You'll experience slow flight control response as just enough airflow is going over the top of the wing to support lift. The aircraft may feel "sluggish" to your inputs.

Throughout your training, you'll be introduced to a variety of emergency procedures. These range from losing radios to using a fire extinguisher and even the rare engine failure. Learning to handle the unexpected loss of engine power in flight is a crucial element of your training. If this happens, the airplane doesn't fall out of the sky. It basically becomes a glider and there are procedures to follow to maintain controllability while finding a suitable landing area and attempting to restart the engine. It is all very manageable and the steps will become automatic to you with repetition. Repetition is the mother of skill! Let me point out that statistics show that U.S. aircraft accidents make up less than 0.15 percent of all transportation fatalities. In fact, 2020 data shows that there were only 5.57 general aviation accidents per every 100,000 flight hours.

Preparation is something the average pilot often neglects but a master pilot does before every flight. Strive to be a master pilot! Continuous practice of emergency procedures gives you the tools to be better prepared to handle any issue that may arise. I often hear from members of the MzeroA Nation how lessons learned from our training has made their response to real world incidents or emergencies automatic. In other words, it helped them save their lives. This is one of the great joys of my career, and the oxygen for me to keep making new content every week for our ground school members and our social media channels.

You'll spend a lot of time in the airport traffic pattern, which is a rectangular course around the airport, usually flown about 1000 feet above ground level (AGL). In this circuit, you have the departure leg, crosswind, downwind, base, and final approach legs. Here is the opportunity to put the ground reference maneuvers, stall prevention and landing practice to work. You'll do several landings per flight until you become safe and proficient.

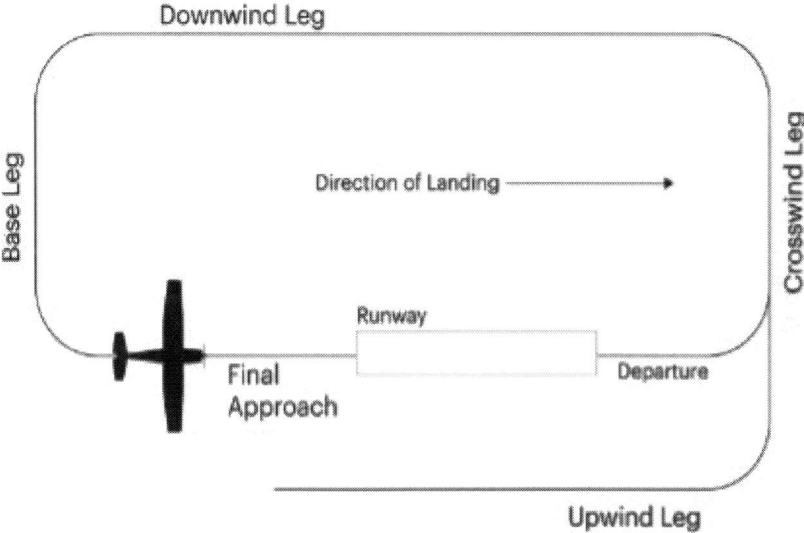

As you progress, your instructor will transfer more duties over to you. This will include talking on the radio and making position reports to other aircraft in the area. This can be a "stage fright" moment for many, but after some role playing and practicing at home, radio communications will come naturally.

Once you become proficient in all of these areas, often another instructor will fly with you and conduct a "stage check," to confirm with your instructor that you are ready to solo.

YOUR FIRST SOLO

You will never forget the day of your first solo! This is your big day when your instructor gets out of the airplane, and you accomplish several takeoffs and landings all by yourself! A first solo flight is a momentous occasion for any pilot and is an amazing accomplishment! There is no FAA-mandated minimum number of flight hours to solo, just an age requirement of 16 years.

Many flight school walls are emblazoned with shirt tails cut off as a tradition for students completing their first solo flight. Aviation lore states that long before aircraft were equipped with radios and headsets to talk with each other, pilots couldn't communicate especially well. The instructor, who sat behind the student in a tandem airplane, would pull at the students shirt to instruct which way to turn. A pull on the left of your shirt tail meant a turn to the left. When the student no longer needed instruction and was ready to solo, the instructor would cut the tail off of the student's shirt, symbolizing that instruction was no longer needed. It's a long standing tradition that continues to this day. You may not want to wear your favorite shirt though the day you solo!

> **REAL WORLD TIP**
>
> A few things to remember before your solo.
> There is a big difference in takeoff performance when your instructor steps out of the airplane. Why? Simply because the airplane will be flying lighter with you alone, than with you and the instructor. I'm close to 200lbs so my students say that when I step out of the airplane it climbs like a rocket!
>
> There is also a big difference in landing. Without that extra weight, you'll have a tendency to "float" down the runway leaving your point of intended landing a few hundred feet behind you.

Remember that your instructor would not have signed you off to solo if she/he didn't truly believe you were ready! After all, they are responsible for you, the aircraft and keeping their instructor certificate. Soloing a student is a BIG responsibility for every CFI!

CROSS COUNTRY PLANNING

Cross country doesn't literally mean flying across the United States in a small airplane. It consists of planning and flying to an airport at least 50 nautical miles from your original place of departure. You will work closely with your flight instructor to plan and complete a cross country prior to accomplishing this task by yourself.

You'll learn more about different types of airspace, minimum weather requirements, flight planning, aircraft performance charts as well as emergency and contingency operations such as what to do if you get lost on the flight. If you haven't already done so, you will conduct flights at an airport with an air traffic control (ATC) tower, further improving your radio communications.

Selecting ground landmarks correctly is crucial in this phase, as you rely solely on visual references for navigation. Ground checkpoints can be cities, rivers, highways, or other prominent landmarks that you can use to compare with your aeronautical chart to ensure you're on the correct course. You'll work with a flight computer to work on basic time, speed, and distance calculations, as well as wind correction angles both in the preflight planning phase and inflight to ensure you're progressing according to plan.

SOLO CROSS COUNTRY

All of the practice and work you did with your instructor throughout your cross country training all leads up to this next adventure.

Your instructor will thoroughly prepare you for this step and endorse you when you are ready. After your instructor reviews your cross country planning and the weather with you, you will set off on this cross country all by yourself! Enjoy this moment and be proud of all you have accomplished. There is something very peaceful and satisfying about flying solo. You now have the skills and ability to fly this airplane and make good decisions about the flight all by yourself.

During the cross-country phase, look down at the ground and recall how you once looked up at the sky, wishing you could fly. This is why you're flying, to go places, to see things and explore this newfound freedom. Enjoy the journey!

PUTTING IT ALL TOGETHER

Each lesson stage builds on the previous one and when they are all complete, it's simply a matter of putting it all together to prepare for your practical test. All areas of training will be evaluated by an FAA examiner on your checkride, so your skills need to be sharp. You will continue to work with your instructor to fine tune any maneuvers or skills as needed. You'll also be applying those skills into more advanced procedures and correlating them into each phase of flight.

After being evaluated by another instructor as a mock checkride, you will be endorsed, or signed off, to take your practical test. We will delve deeper into what you'll experience during the checkride in Chapter 6.

CHAPTER 5
KEYS TO THE KNOWLEDGE TEST

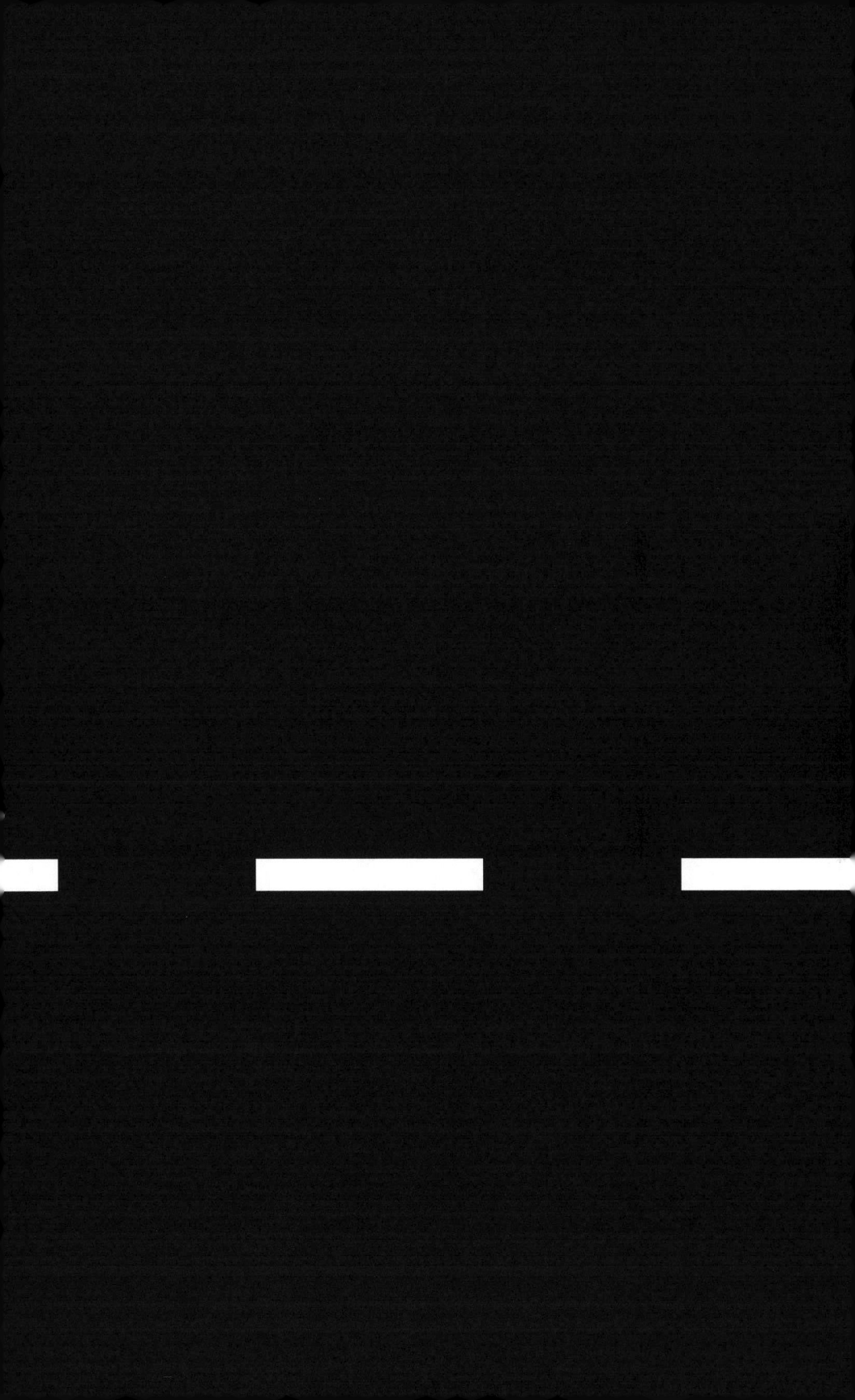

CHAPTER 5
Keys to the Knowledge Test

"Mystery creates wonder and wonder is the basis of man's desire to understand."

-Neil Armstrong

We've spent some time discussing the fun part of your training, the flying portion, but there's another area that we need to discuss: the FAA Knowledge Test. You'll take this written test at some point in your training, after your ground school is completed and, preferably before you begin the actual flight training. You will need it prior to taking your checkride.

The material for the Knowledge Test is covered in the MzeroA Online Ground School, with a detailed list of topics available in 14 CFR 61.105. A key reference book you will often need is the FAR/AIM. The first half of this book, the Federal Aviation Regulations (FAR), contains many pertinent regulations and information. You can find 14 CFR 61.105 and many others in the FAR section of this book. The second half of the book is the Aeronautical Information Manual (AIM), which explains topics in a plain language format and uses illustrations for better understanding. Subject areas on the written test range from regulations to weight and balance, and aerodynamics just to name a few.

Learners must schedule ahead to take the written test. Know that tests are administered by an independent testing center and locations can be found online. You'll have 2 hours 30 minutes to answer 60 multiple choice questions on a computer with a proctor present at the testing site. Often your flight school may have a testing center located on the airport. The average price to take the test is between $150-$200 depending on location. It's a very controlled environment, where cellphones, tablets, etc. are not allowed into the testing room with you. Some people like to bring their own calculator for the written test but just be aware that scientific calculators are not allowed. You can ask your testing center about any restrictions when you schedule your test.

You'll need to bring a photo ID and items like your flight computer and an endorsement from an instructor certifying that you possess the required ground knowledge to take the written test. MzeroA automatically issues this endorsement upon your successful completion of our Online Ground School. The testing center supplies you with the Private Pilot Airman Knowledge Testing Supplement so you can reference the figures during your test.

REAL WORLD TIP

MzeroA members score 6 points higher on their FAA exams when compared to the national average.

The FAA takes measures to ensure that no one has access to their entire database. Questions and answer choices are frequently updated to eliminate test question memorization. This is why it is so important to use a ground school that avoids rote memorization and focuses on the understanding of the material and concepts. The wording of test questions can sometimes be tricky. You must know how to apply what you learned to any given scenario or question. It is a knowledge test, NOT a "who can memorize the most questions" test. In order to be a safe, competent pilot-in-command, and to pass the required tests, there are no shortcuts. You must acquire the necessary pilot knowledge and apply what you have learned to successfully pass the test with at least a 70%. This success is achievable through the MzeroA Aviation Mastery Method, used by hundreds of thousands of pilots.

The private pilot course in the MzeroA Online Ground School is broken down into different lessons. Each lesson is then broken down into different video topics you will encounter along your journey to become a private pilot. Rather than reading the material alone, our videos explain it in an easy-to-understand format. This aids in learning and comprehending each topic and leads to a deeper level of understanding. Every lesson has a quiz at the end with a multitude of available questions. You can take each quiz an unlimited amount of times. This repetition helps with the mastery of the material. MzeroA makes sure that you'll be well prepared to pass the test with flying colors!

WHEN AM I READY?

By the time you've completed your ground school, you should feel confident in your ability to pass the test. If you have any questions or are struggling with understanding a specific topic, seek additional instruction from a qualified instructor. The MzeroA support team can help! Our team successfully answers thousands of questions every year from students around the world about any aviation topic one could imagine.

When you take practice tests, you'll typically score high. The information will be fresh in your mind and you will be practicing in a comfortable environment. We want you to be familiar with the testing format, so we've built a test center emulator into our online ground school. We have even injected the science of learning in the format of the practice final exams so that the page mimics the experience of the actual testing center. This will give you an edge when taking the actual exam because you will know what to expect.

Even though you'll be well prepared, scores on the actual knowledge test tend to be lower than your practice tests. Nerves are a contributing factor. Prior to scheduling and taking your actual FAA Knowledge test, you should score in the mid to high 90s on each of your practice final exams before taking the real thing. Although no one is perfect, there have been several people who have scored an impressive 100% on their FAA written exam. Many of the perfect score achievers are MzeroA Ground School members! It is possible. In addition to the ground school, take advantage of all the FREE material MzeroA offers online. Information on some of the most important subjects you will be tested on is free to you by just subscribing to the MzeroA Flight Training YouTube channel, social media pages and podcasts. Keep in mind that your written test score will directly influence the difficulty level of the oral portion of your checkride.

At the end of your flight training, you'll take your practical test (checkride). The FAA practical test is two parts, an oral exam and a flight check. During the oral exam, the examiner will ask you verbal questions related to items missed on the written exam. If you walk into the checkride with a knowledge test score in the 70s range, it shows the evaluator that you have significant deficiencies in your knowledge. You can expect to spend more time being questioned in those areas during the checkride since the examiner needs to determine if you have the knowledge and skills to be a safe pilot. However, if you walk into the checkride with a strong 90% or better, the evaluator knows that you are competent. Shoot for the moon here!

CHAPTER 6
PASS YOUR CHECKRIDE

CHAPTER 6
Pass your Checkride

"At the moment of truth, there are either reasons or results."
-Chuck Yeager

The day of your private pilot practical test (checkride) is rapidly approaching. You've invested valuable time and money preparing for the moment. You may even feel nervous and stressed, wondering how your first encounter with an FAA examiner will be. Feeling anxious is normal! Remember, if an instructor has endorsed you for the checkride, they believe you are ready—it's their job to know. Today, you drop 'student' from 'student pilot.'

If you are enjoying this book, take note that I wrote another book entirely dedicated to helping you pass your checkride called Pass Your Private Pilot Checkride. In it you will find many of the examiners' favorite checkride questions and the answers to better prepare you for your big day.

Either the FAA or an FAA Designated Pilot Examiner (DPE) will conduct your practical test. Often, FAA inspectors are busy with other duties, so a DPE will take their place. DPEs are not randomly assigned. They are independent and often have a working relationship with various flight schools. Your flight school will likely have a list of local DPEs for most of their checkrides. Each DPE charges a fee, allowing you to choose who administers your checkride.

WHAT TO EXPECT

As mentioned earlier, The FAA Private Pilot Airman Certification Standards (ACS) sets the requirements and tolerances for each flight maneuver as well as topics, known as tasks, that can be covered during your checkride. This is a document that you should familiarize yourself with before the practical test.

Preparing for all areas listed in the ACS will not only help you ace the checkride but make you a better real world pilot.

The oral portion of the practical test helps the examiner determine whether the applicant is sufficiently prepared to advance to the flight portion of the practical test. However, questioning will continue throughout the entire practical test. This is the time when you will be asked questions from some of the areas that you gave incorrect answers on the written test.

During the ground and flight portion of the practical test, the FAA requires examiners to assess your mastery of the topics. In certain cases, the examiner will ask the applicant to describe or explain a concept. At other times, the examiner will assess the applicant's understanding through scenario based questions. This requires you to appropriately apply knowledge and experience to real-world scenarios. For example, scenario based questions may be similar to "what if your GPS failed here?" or "Can you fly into this type of airspace?"

The examiner often requires you to have a flight planned in advance for a cross country. This will be used as a base for examination. I recommend that you arrive at your checkride with the whole plan not only on your tablet or phone, but also with a back-up in place. This redundancy showcases your thoughtful preparation and attention to safety. We all know that batteries fail and technology doesn't always work as it should.

You'll review the aircraft maintenance logs, your weight and balance calculations as well as your personal pilot logbook. Your instructor will do a final review of your logbook prior, to make sure you meet all requirements. Nothing is more embarrassing than arriving for a checkride and not having all the criteria met. This flight plan part of the checkride is designed to be conversational, NOT confrontational.

Don't be afraid if you can't remember something. You can be assured the examiner knows the right answer, so it is not a good idea to try and bluff an answer. Instead, ask to refer to your aviation library. You can bring all your notes and FAR/AIM to your checkride. Knowing where to find the correct answer and asking to look it up will often satisfy the evaluator. Be sure to have the most up to date FAR/AIM book and sectional charts with you. In order to remain current, you must use the latest revisions of all information.

The flight portion of the practical test requires the applicant to demonstrate knowledge, risk management, flight proficiency, and operational skill in accordance with the ACS. You may start off on the cross country flight you previously planned, and the examiner may ask you to divert to another airport. Once those tasks are satisfactorily completed, you will perform all the air work that you have practiced to proficiency during your training. Finally, you will proceed to an airport for the takeoffs and landings portion of the evaluation.

OUTCOMES

In order to calm your nerves, know that the examiner wants you to pass. The examiner has no quotas for pass/fail rates. They want to see that you are a safe, competent, and knowledgeable pilot. However, the objectives are clearly stated in the ACS and they must be met. There are three possible outcomes of the practical test:

- Temporary Airman Certificate (satisfactory)
- Letter of Discontinuance
- Notice of Disapproval (unsatisfactory)

TEMPORARY AIRMAN CERTIFICATE

If you perform satisfactorily in all testing areas, you will be issued a Temporary Airman Certificate. It is called a temporary because it is a paper version but you should know that a hard copy will arrive later to you in the mail. At that point, you will destroy the temporary and carry the hard copy with you. This is what you have worked so hard for and is quite an achievement. Congratulations, you have earned your Private Pilot Certificate! MzeroA strives to have this be the outcome for all our students!

LETTER OF DISCONTINUANCE

Let's say you successfully complete the ground portion of the oral exam but the weather isn't ideal, the aircraft has mechanical issues, or you become ill, you will not be able to complete the flight portion of your checkride. Things happen and perhaps you decide not to fly that day. You will be issued a Letter of Discontinuance which means you're satisfactory up to that point and you'll pick up later where you stopped. This is NOT a failure but a formal means to issue a raincheck on the checkride.

> **REAL WORLD TIP**
>
> If an applicant receives a Notice of Disapproval or Letter of Discontinuance, he or she may receive credit for items passed, but only within a 60 day period after the first date of disapproval or discontinuance. You don't have to redo the passed parts if you retest within 60 days. However, if not complete in that time-frame, you must redo the entire test.

NOTICE OF DISAPPROVAL

If the examiner determines that a task is incomplete, uncertain, or unsafe, they will require you to repeat that task or a portion of it. If the outcome of the second attempt is unsatisfactory, the examiner must issue a Notice of Disapproval. This is known as a "bust" or checkride failure.

WHAT CONSTITUTES A "BUST"?

Typical areas of unsatisfactory performance include:

- Any action or lack of action by the applicant that requires corrective intervention by the evaluator to maintain safe flight
- Failure to use proper and effective visual scanning

techniques to clear the area before and while performing maneuvers
- Consistently exceeding tolerances stated in the skill elements of the task
- Failure to take prompt corrective action when tolerances are exceeded
- Failure to exercise risk management

These are very straightforward, and they eliminate ambiguity. Consistently exceeding tolerances is self- explanatory. If the examiner must intervene to maintain safety, that's also a big issue. Since a Private Pilot Certificate is flying by visual references, not ensuring the airspace is safe and free of other aircraft before each maneuver is another clear example of unsatisfactory performance. Reviewing the ACS standards prior to the practical test will give you a good idea of all expectations.

The examiner is essentially your first passenger. Treat them that way. Do everything exactly the way you've done it during your training including the mock checkride. Take the time to give a proper passenger briefing, explain that you will be looking for traffic and if they see another airplane, to let you know. Enjoy the ride and most importantly remember that you are the Pilot in Command! Don't be afraid to make decisions or speak up if you see something unusual.

It's often easier said than done but try and relax! Obtaining your Private Pilot Certificate is something to be very proud of, and it takes hard work. Passing your checkride is the beginning!

CHAPTER 7
THE SKY'S THE LIMIT

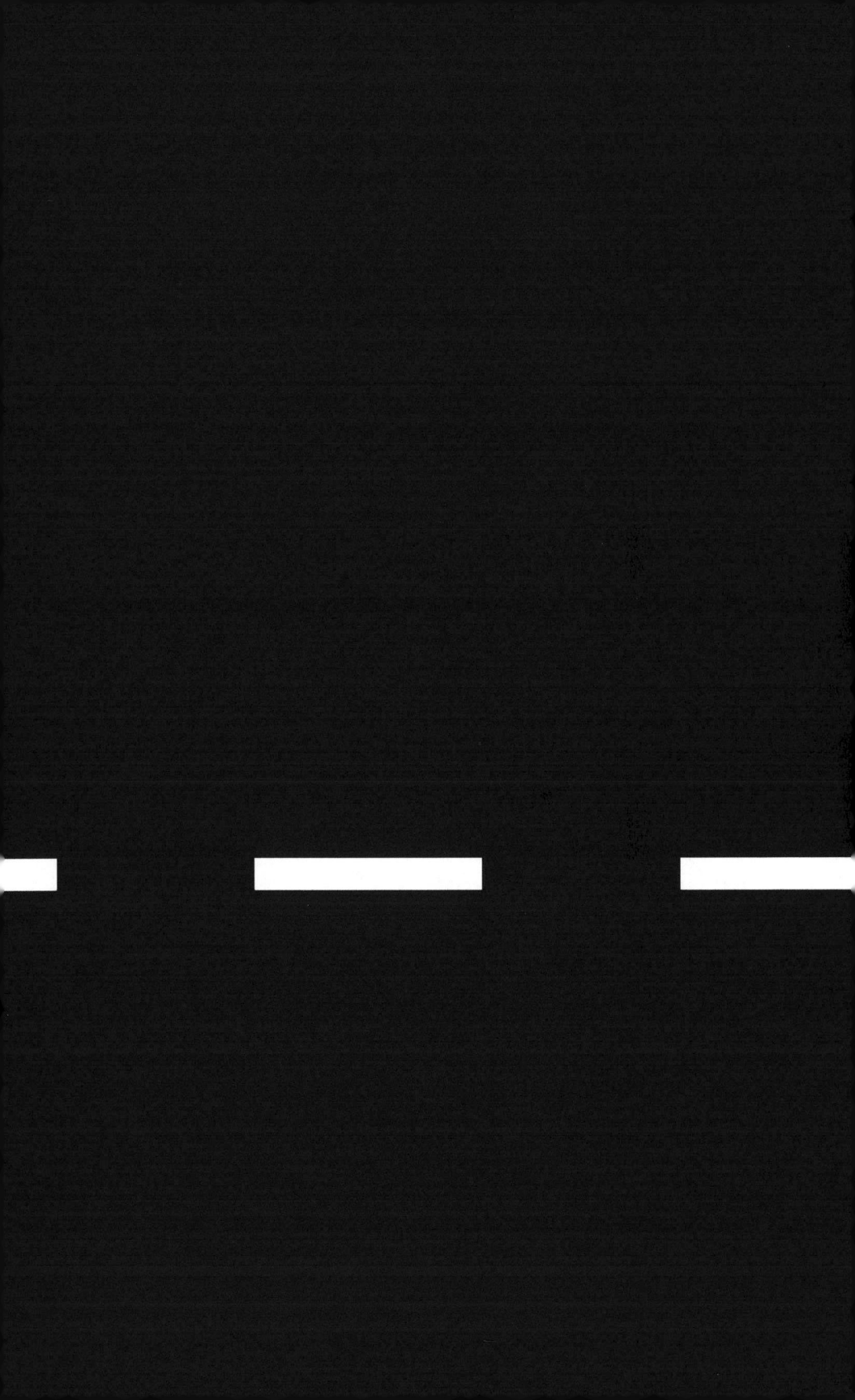

CHAPTER 7
The Sky's the Limit

Aviation is proof that given the will, we have the capacity to achieve the impossible.

-Edward Vernon Rickenbacker

Congratulations! You have just accomplished an amazing goal! Enjoy this new privilege. Some private pilots are satisfied with this level of achievement. You can now take friends and family flying and enjoy taking trips on good visual weather days. However, there are more flying opportunities beyond earning your Private Pilot Certificate.

INSTRUMENT RATING

The most common next step after obtaining a Private Pilot certificate is to earn an instrument rating. "If you're considering a career in aviation, frequently fly in less than perfect weather, or seek more air traffic control services for added safety, you will need this rating. If you plan to own an airplane, an instrument rating will even help lower insurance rates. You'll receive training and additional instruction in various types of weather—even inside the clouds! Additionally, an instrument rating is required for all flights operating in Class A airspace (at

18,000 feet and above) and also required when operating under Special Visual Flight Rules (SVFR) at night. MzeroA prepares thousands of private pilots a year to earn their instrument rating. Even if you never plan on using it, it gives you a safety net to use if you ever get in an unexpected situation with marginal weather. Many times I've been flying VFR with clear skies and beautiful sunshine, then unexpected weather moves in and I'm very thankful I have my IFR skillset and rating.

COMMERCIAL PILOT

If you aspire to have a professional aviation career, the next step after your Instrument rating is the Commercial Pilot Certificate. As a commercial pilot, you can now be paid or compensated to fly passengers or cargo. Commercial pilots must be at least 18 years of age, receive additional training, and pass both a knowledge and a practical test. Some of the maneuvers you demonstrated during your private pilot checkride will be required, but they must be done to higher standards. New performance maneuvers will be introduced along with new regulations pertaining to flying for hire. You'll need more flight experience to become eligible for the Commercial Pilot Certificate, but for a career in aviation, this is a necessity.

AIRCRAFT TRANSITION TRAINING

Technically Advanced Aircraft

One of the most common and exciting opportunities is learning to fly a more advanced aircraft. Perhaps during initial flight training, you chose a less expensive aircraft to conduct your training. Now may be the time to do a rental checkout with an instructor and change airplanes.

You may consider transitioning to what is known as a 'glass cockpit,' which features computerized display screens instead of traditional gauges. These aircraft have computerized screens rather than individual gauges. Technically Advanced Aircraft (TAA) are becoming more and more prevalent in general aviation. Maybe you were flying an older model Cessna 172 with traditional "six-pack steam gauges" and want to move to a Garmin G1000 equipped aircraft. Obtaining transition training is a smart choice to learn the new equipment.

High Performance Aircraft

Federal Aviation Regulations require pilots to have a high-performance endorsement to act as pilot-in- command (PIC) of a high-performance airplane which is any airplane with an engine capable of producing more than 200 horsepower. This one-time logbook endorsement can be earned through ground and flight training. This typically consists of a 1-2 hour ground school session and 3-5 hours in the airplane to learn the nuances of high performance aircraft. You'll learn about the systems and how to manage the aircraft in a typically faster pace environment which is common in high performance flying.

Complex Endorsement

A complex airplane features retractable landing gear, flaps, and a controllable pitch propeller. This includes aircraft equipped with systems like FADEC, which uses a computer to control the engine and propeller. Sounds complex, doesn't it? By the time you get to this point in your training, it will make more sense. This is another one-time logbook endorsement involving ground and flight training. The ground portion is usually 1-2 hours and the flight training can range from about 4-8 hours of instruction. Most flight schools have a minimum flight hour requirement in this particular type of airplane, normally 10-15 hours, before allowing a pilot to rent a complex aircraft for other than receiving instruction. This is typically for insurance purposes and it's a wise decision since there are new systems to learn and manage

Add a Rating

Known as an "add-on", pilots often add or build onto an existing pilot certificate to exercise more privileges. They keep learning. A certificate authorizes a pilot to fly and be pilot in command under that certification. For example, we already discussed private and commercial certificates. They each have different privileges and limitations. Along with those allowances, a certificated pilot also has the choice to add onto that certificate by adding privileges such as an instrument rating, which allows you to fly in clouds or low visibility. Pilots may want to add on a multi-engine rating, which allows the pilot to fly an airplane with more than one engine. Let's look deeper into some of these opportunities.

Seaplane Rating

Many pilots report that earning a seaplane rating is the most enjoyable flying experience they have had. There are several types of seaplanes: float planes, flying boats, and amphibious aircraft. Float planes are supported by floats which keep the plane above the water when it lands. A flying boat is different in that its body is shaped like the hull of a boat. The hull actually rests on the water's surface when it lands. Amphibious aircraft are able to land on both water and land. There are many locations that offer seaplane ratings across the U.S. in a variety of different aircraft. There is no specific flight time minimum requirement for earning a seaplane rating if you already have your airplane single engine land certification. Typically, a pilot can expect 5 hours of training to gain proficiency and then complete a required checkride to earn the rating.

Multi Engine Rating

Flying an aircraft with more than one engine requires a multi-engine rating. For many, earning a multi-engine rating is their first experience performing pilot duties in a complex aircraft. These new systems can present new procedural challenges and new systems and concepts including multi engine aerodynamics, rules governing certification of multi engine aircraft, and unique engine failure scenarios, such as safely shutting an engine down in flight.

In most cases it makes more sense to wait until a pilot has a commercial pilot certificate or at least an instrument rating to earn a multi engine rating. It is an advanced system aircraft that is often used in commercial operations or other charter flying careers. There are no minimum flight time requirements for the multi-engine land rating nor is there a required written test. Typically, it takes about 10-15 hours of flight training, and passing a checkride, to earn your multi-engine rating.

OTHER CERTIFICATES

Remote Pilot

The use of small Unmanned Aircraft Systems (sUAS) is expected to continue increasing globally for the foreseeable future. These are commonly referred to as drones and to be able to legally operate these commercially for hire, you will need a Remote Pilot Certificate. This allows you to operate under Part 107 of the Federal Aviation Regulations.

Remote pilot, commercial drone pilot, or sUAS pilots are all terms often used interchangeably when discussing the certificate.

There are two types of applicants for the Remote Pilot Certificate: those who already hold an FAA-issued pilot certificate (excluding student pilots) and those who do not. Your pilot certificate must be current. This means that you had a flight review or newly acquired rating within the past 24 calendar months. If you meet these requirements, there is a fast track course available online to become a remote pilot. If you do not meet these two requirements, you are a non-pilot applicant. The differentiation lies within the training and application process.

> **REAL WORLD TIP**
>
> Did you know that there are many job opportunities for drone pilots? Careers exist in real estate, photography, tower or building inspections, law enforcement, military, delivery or monitoring of farm operations just to name a few!

As a non-pilot applicant, you'll need to complete a knowledge test. While an instructor endorsement isn't needed, the aeronautical knowledge is similar to the requirements to become a private pilot. MzeroA has a complete online training course to pass the Remote Pilot knowledge test. Thousands of current remote pilots have used the MzeroA Remote Pilot course to successfully pass the FAA Knowledge Test and become safe and well trained remote pilots. See for yourself by visiting MzeroA.com and click on the unmanned link for more information. The QR code below will also take you to the website for remote pilot training.

Airline Transport Pilot

As previously mentioned, while a Commercial Pilot Certificate allows for compensated flying, an Airline Transport Pilot (ATP) Certificate is the highest level of pilot certification required for airline operations. An ATP is the highest level of pilot certification. The ATP is required to fly for an airline or as a charter captain.

You'll need to be at least 23 years of age to become an ATP and meet the training and experience requirements. Typically, this includes 1,500 hours of total flight time, however, there are some accelerated routes through the military or some collegiate aviation programs that come with certain restrictions but require less flight hours. Just like other certificates, the ATP requires a knowledge and practical test, as well as some additional training requirements for the multi-engine ATP including receiving training in an advanced flight simulator.

Flight Instructor

"If you aim for a career in aviation, consider becoming a Certificated Flight Instructor (CFI) to deepen your understanding and accumulate flight hours. There's no better way to really learn and understand something until you teach it. If you want to make flying a career, becoming a CFI is a great way to build flight experience while honing your people skills. The possibilities are endless! The good news is that MzeroA will be by your side and as we like to say, "A good pilot is always learning."

CHAPTER 8
THE AVIATION MASTERY METHOD

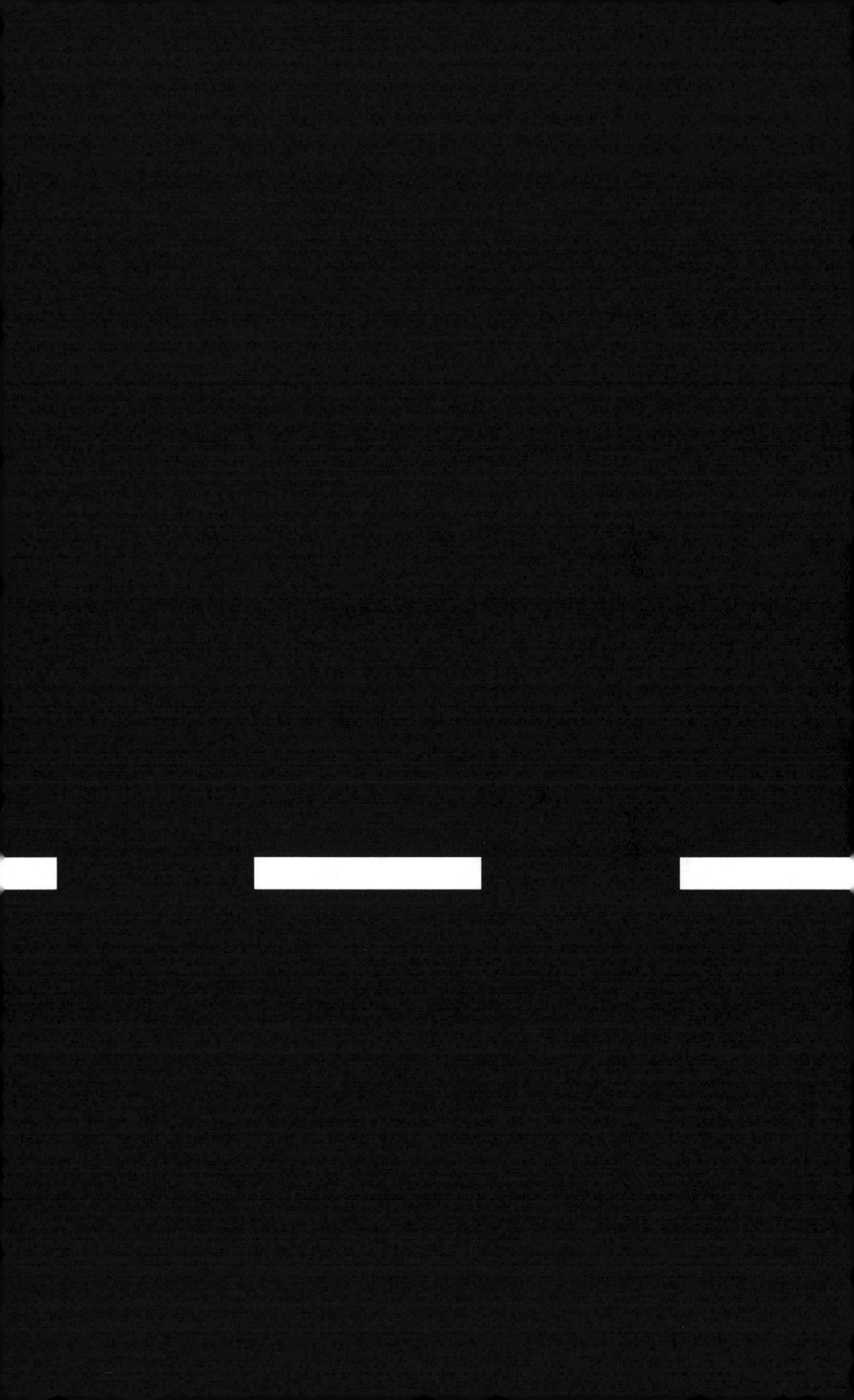

CHAPTER 8
The Aviation Mastery Method

"A good pilot is always learning."

-Jason Schappert

We've highlighted key experiences on your journey to becoming a pilot. I'm often asked for advice on how to succeed in aviation. This underscores a point I've made before: the airplane is an expensive classroom. Completing some sort of ground school will save you time and money on your aviation journey.

> **REAL WORLD TIP**
>
> Learn everything you can when you are on the ground.

We've also stressed the importance of ground training which will lead to your success along the way. It's imperative that you have proficiency in your flying skills and your aeronautical knowledge. Proficiency in areas like aircraft operations, systems, weather, weight and balance, airspace, navigation, regulations, and emergency procedures will make you a safe and knowledgeable pilot.

You may be asking yourself, how can I possibly learn all these things? And, "Why should I choose MzeroA over another ground school provider?" The answer is easy.

At MzeroA, we've successfully helped over 130,000 pilots pass both their knowledge and practical tests. We base our instruction on the science of learning to create true learning both in the air and on the ground. Unlike other programs that focus solely on rote memorization for the written tests, we ensure you understand the concepts through real-world training. It's not just a memorization marathon or a crash course. We also use the latest technology to keep our courses current, accurate and relevant. We strive to encourage and inspire pilots to be the best they can be.

Each section of every MzeroA course is broken down into more manageable lessons that make it easy to follow and a methodical order that covers exactly what you need to know in order to pass your FAA knowledge and practical test and much more. What you learn here will be used throughout all your flying. As we like to say, it's the real-world applicability that we teach and that ultimately makes you a safer, smarter pilot.

Additionally, unlike other courses on the market, the MzeroA team is always in the studio and the airplane filming new content, and we are always creating innovative ways to deliver training and valuable information to you.

MzeroA operates on a membership model, giving you access to all our manned aviation courses for a single monthly fee, available whenever you need it. Because we are always creating new training content, many members keep their subscriptions for years. Remember- A good pilot is always learning!

Perhaps you're a private pilot who wants to look ahead at the instrument pilot content; or you're working on your commercial certificate and need to refresh your private and instrument knowledge: MzeroA offers access to all courses for one small monthly membership price.

MzeroA members have access to weekly webinars, and over 1,000 full flight training videos so you can know exactly what to expect in the airplane before you fly.

If you need help during a course, our dedicated team of FAA-certificated flight instructors is ready to assist you via live chat, email, and phone support. Indeed, you will speak directly with a flight instructor, not a call center operator.

We can tell you with confidence that MzeroA is the best resource out there to pass the FAA Knowledge Test, checkride and most importantly make you a safer real- world pilot. We don't expect you to just take our word for it. That's why we offer a full 30-day, no questions asked, money back guarantee. If that's not enough, we want you to try us with no obligation! We offer a free trial to check out our courses and experience the MzeroA difference first-hand.

"Explore our free trial to see firsthand if our approach and teaching style meet your needs. Review the material at your leisure, and if you find it's not right for you, simply let us know. Just let us know within 30 days of signing up and we'll refund your money, no questions asked!

By now, we hope that most of your questions are answered and you're convinced that you can accomplish your dream of becoming a pilot and MzeroA offers a clear path in which to do so. The MzeroA team is with you every step of the way. Together, we'll climb higher as you pursue aviation mastery!

OTHER TITLES BY JASON SCHAPPERT

Pass your Private Pilot Checkride

Pass your Instrument Pilot Checkride

Pass your Commercial Pilot Checkride

Aviation Mastery

APPENDIX
Aviation Acronyms

A&P	-	Airframe and Powerplant Mechanic
ACS	-	Airframe and Powerplant Mechanic
ADIZ	-	Air Defense Identification Zone
AGL	-	Above Ground Level
AIM	-	Aeronautical Information Manual
AME	-	Aviation Medical Examiner
ARTCC	-	Air Route Traffic Control Center
ASOS	-	Automatic Surface Observation System
ATC	-	Air Traffic Control
ATD	-	Aviation Training Device
ATIS	-	Automated Terminal Information Service
ATP	-	Airline Transport Pilot
CFI	-	Certificated Flight Instructor
CFIT	-	Controlled Flight Into Terrain
CFR	-	Code of Federal Regulations
CRM	-	Crew Resource Management
DH	-	Decision Height
DME	-	Distance Measuring Equipment
DP	-	Departure Procedure
DPE	-	Designated Pilot Examiner
ETA	-	Estimated Time of Arrival
ETE	-	Estimated Time En Route
FAA	-	Federal Aviation Administration
FADEC	-	Full Authority Digital Engine Control
FL	-	Flight Level
FP	-	Flight Plan
FSS	-	Flight Service Station
FTSP	-	Flight Training Security Program

GA	-	General Aviation
GPS	-	Global Positioning System
IA	-	Inspection Authorization
ICAO	-	International Civil Aviation Organization
ILS	-	Instrument Landing System
IMC	-	Instrument Meteorological Conditions
LAHSO	-	Land and Hold Short Operations
LOC	-	Localizer
LORAN	-	Long Range Aid to Navigation
MALS	-	Medium Intensity Approach Lighting System
MALSF	-	MALS with Sequenced Flashers
MALSR	-	MALS with Runway Alignment Indicator
MAP	-	Missed Approach Point
MCA	-	Minimum Crossing Altitude
MDA	-	Minimum Descent Altitude
MEA	-	Minimum En Route Altitude
METAR	-	Meteorological Aerodrome Report
MOA	-	Military Operations Area
MOCA	-	Minimum Obstruction Clearance Altitude
MSA	-	Minimum Safe Altitude
MSL	-	Mean Sea Level
MVFR	-	Marginal Visual Flight Rules
NEXRAD	-	Next Generation Weather Radar
NOAA	-	National Oceanic & Atmospheric Administration
NOTAM	-	Notice to Air Mission
NTSB	-	National Transportation Safety Board
NWS	-	National Weather Service
PAPI	-	Precision Approach Path Indicator
PAR	-	Precision Approach Radar
PIC	-	Pilot in Command

PIREP	-	Pilot Report
RAIM	-	Receiver Autonomous Integrity Monitoring
REIL	-	Runway End Identification Lights
RNAV	-	Area Navigation
SIC	-	Second in Command
SID	-	Standard Instrument Departure
STAR	-	Standard Terminal Arrival Route
SVFR	-	Special Visual Flight Rules
TAA	-	Technically Advanced Aircraft
TACAN	-	Tactical Aircraft Control and Navigation
TAF	-	Terminal Area Forecast
TCAS	-	Terrain and Collision Avoidance System
TSA	-	Transportation Security Administration
UAS	-	Unmanned Aerial Systems
UNICOM	-	Universal Integrated Communications
VASI	-	Visual Approach Slope Indicator
VFR	-	Visual Flight Rules
VHF	-	Very High Frequency
VMC	-	Visual Meteorological Conditions
VOR	-	VHF Omnidirectional Range
VORTAC	-	VOR collocated with TACAN
VOT	-	VOR Test Facility
WAAS	-	Wide Area Augmentation System
WX	-	Weather

NOTES

NOTES

NOTES

Made in the USA
Las Vegas, NV
07 November 2024